Deployment to Employment

A guide for military veterans transitioning to civilian employment

RUSS HOVENDICK

Faithful Life Publishers & Printers
North Fort Myers, FL 33903

FaithfulLifePublishers.com

Deployment to Employment

ISBN: 978-1-937129-86-6

Directional Motivation, LLC.
5421 W 41st #202
Sioux Falls, SD 57106

(605) 362-8176 ext 101
russ@directionalmotivation.com

Published and printed by:
Faithful Life Publishers & Printers
3335 Galaxy Way
North Fort Myers, FL 33903

888.720.0950

www.FaithfulLifePublishers.com
info@FaithfulLifePublishers.com

Printed in the United States of America.

18 17 16 15 14 13 1 2 3 4 5

DEDICATION

I humbly dedicate this book to the late Lt. Col. Mark Weber, whose passion for life, his family, and his military community serves as a shining example of how to live with purpose and find fulfillment.

Back in December 2012, I was introduced to Mark and approached him about writing the foreword for this book. "What the hell," he said. "Sure, bring it on. But you better hurry, as my clock is running at mach speed!" Unfortunately, Mark's clock wound down far faster than anyone would have wished. He died on June 13, 2013.

I was privileged to know Mark for only several months, yet he had a profound influence on me and my efforts to help vets. For him, motivating veterans was personal. He was noticeably frustrated, even angered, that too many veterans had given up on finding jobs. In every conversation we had, I felt his explosive energy. If he could take every unemployed veteran who had lost hope and scream at them until they realized they had what it took to succeed, he certainly would have tried.

Deployment to Employment, borne out of my desire to contribute something vital and meaningful to our nation's military veterans, is a product of Mark's influence on me. He once pointed out my tenacity in lifting up veterans. "I admire your pluck," he once wrote to me.

At the time, I didn't know what he meant, so I looked it up. *Merriam-Webster Dictionary* defines it as "courageous readiness to fight or continue against odds: dogged resolution."[1]

My sincere thanks to you, Mark, for your tremendous contribution to my life and to this book. Through your writing and speaking, you allowed all of us bystanders to see life through your eyes. You faced death with grace and an open heart and continued to fight for veterans in your last days. That took an enormous amount of pluck.

---

1 *Merriam-Webster Dictionary*, http://www.merriam-webster.com/dictionary/pluck.

BOOK REVIEWS

I've been a federal veterans service representative, VA military service coordinator, and U.S. Marine. Not only have I've personally gone through the rough transition from military service to private sector employment, I've also seen dozens of others going through it. Russ has produced a tool that bridges the "misunderstanding gap" between private sector employers and military veterans. This is a tremendous resource, needed by every transitioning veteran. I recommend reading this book with a pen and paper on standby.

— Nolan Ruby, former Marine Corps sergeant

I can relate to the obstacles of transitioning after a long career in the military. Those of us that have served in the armed forces for over twenty-five years have centered our lives on military philosophies and work ethics. We strive for integrity, honor, and courage, and we commit each day to the uniform. This is an excellent resource, and I highly recommend this book to all service members transitioning to civilian life.

— Derek L. Hayes, retired Marine Corps master gunnery sergeant

This is an awesome resource. I wish I would've had this book when I first started looking for a new job. In thirty minutes of reading *Deployment to Employment*, I learned what took me months to gather and learn from multiple seminars, resources, business coaches, and others. If you consider yourself a military-minded person, this book was written for you. It gives you the secrets of the civilian way of thinking and teaches you how to translate your military skills to the civilian world. This book should be required reading for all service members approaching their post-military chapter of life.

— Rob Nielsen, former Marine Corps company commander and platoon commander

This book is an invaluable resource for service members transitioning from active duty. I am one year out from my own exit date and already starting to feel apprehensive about it. This book has provided useful exercises and tools to help me prepare for my civilian career.

— Jon L. Carrico, Jr., Army Reserve lieutenant colonel

The first book in the Directional Motivation series was a magnetic read. It caught me and held me throughout. I even began carrying it as I traveled, offering it to friends at very high levels of authority. The second book, *How to Interview,* and now the third, *Deployment to Employment,* have made a greater impact on me. It is clear that the author has an unwavering passion to help military veterans. As a former Marine who spent several decades educating and empowering veterans, I believe this book gives its readers the gift of explosive potential for success.

— Ron Tottingham, Major General SSC – Former Marine

One thing I didn't know leaving the military was how to transition myself into the civilian world. My only battle plan was to keep moving forward. This book gave me a more solid battle plan through positive reinforcement and concrete advice—exactly what I needed.

— David Gould, former Army first sergeant, platoon sergeant

Wow, what can I say, this book is excellent! It's a must-read for military personnel and veterans seeking to significantly increase their odds of landing a great job.

The author not only lays out a clear process for job seekers—he also provides the underlying psychology that drives the process. Even better, the author offers tools for implementing and leveraging each step along the path. As icing on the cake, this book has a warm, down-to-earth quality, which makes it extremely easy to read and follow.

When the author's ingredients for success are mixed together, the result is a powerful message that represents the wisdom of experience. Simply stated, to *get* the right thing, you must *do* the right thing, and to *do* the right thing, you must *know* the right thing. Without a doubt, this book will help you do that.

— Mikel J. Harry, Ph.D., co-creator of Six Sigma

Dr. Harry has been widely recognized as the principal architect of Six Sigma and the world's leading authority in business management. His book *Six Sigma: The Breakthrough Management Strategy Revolutionizing the World's Top Corporations* was listed on the national best seller lists of the *Wall Street Journal*, the *New York Times* and *Business W*eek. He has been a consultant to many of the world's top CEOs such as Jack Welch, former CEO and chairman of General Electric Corporation and Robert "Bob" Galvin, former CEO and chairman of Motorola. Dr. Harry has also been a featured guest on popular television programs such as the premier NBC show *Power Lunch*.

Russ Hovendick has taken his considerable recruiter experience and combined it with a deep personal commitment to understand the true challenges veterans face. Especially unique is his understanding of "who these men and women are" and the challenges they face. Russ provides the reader with action items for their development – key to their understanding "who they are". The importance of this effort is documented in the Preface by Colonel David F. Smith U.S. Army (retired). Every transitioning military person can benefit from the deeply personal, revealing and valuable comments David shares. Russ also brings the perspective of the employer to the transitioning military personnel. I like the focus of the book, its understanding of the veteran and the experienced mentoring Russ offers the reader. I highly recommend this work to every man and woman transitioning from a military career to a purposeful civilian life.

— **Michael** E. **Echols**, Ph.D. Executive Vice President of Strategic Initiatives and the Human Capital Lab, **Bellevue** University

Author "Your Future is Calling, A Practical Guide to the Education You Need to Have the Future You Desire" www.LearnProsper.com

Leader: Veteran Initiative for Advancement (VIA) at Bellevue University www.corporatelearning.com/veterans

ACKNOWLEDGMENTS

From the moment I decided to write this book, I knew that if it didn't speak to the millions of unemployed military veterans and soon-to-be ex-service members, the book would be useless. So my team and I reached out to unemployed veterans and active service members of all types to get a clear understanding of their struggles and the internal blocks holding them back. We also reached out to many ex-military folks who had successfully landed civilian jobs and had valuable insights on their transition.

As I delved deeper into the military mindset, I became more effective at designing job search solutions specifically for ex-service members. Thank you to those from the service who shared your personal stories and life lessons. By helping me gain a deeper understanding of the military experience, you played a major role in the making of this book. I offer a huge thank you to David Smith, a retired colonel from the Army who contributed a deeply personal and inspiring message in the foreword.

My sincere thanks to Millie Lapidario for the countless hours of research and editing to make this book a reality. A special thank you to my son, Darin, for making the book a truly multimedia experience and for your continuing efforts in marketing the book. Darin, you've developed a knack for knowing what's going on in my head and you always manage to help me bring those thoughts to life.

TABLE OF CONTENTS

FOREWORD

Last year marked the end of my thirty years of service in the U.S. Army. As I approached my ETS[2] date, I reflected on my journey, rising from Private E-1 to Colonel.

I recalled my hunger to move up the chain of command. I was definitely proud of my accomplishments, yet more conscious than ever of the sacrifices I had made over three decades. I had pursued multiple opportunities that required me to uproot my life, including a three-year deployment in Egypt in the 1990s during a particularly violent insurgence. I had missed multiple holidays with my family, loved ones' birthdays, even my daughter's birth.

So I figured I deserved to take time off. Before retiring, I told my wife my plan: *I would be a stay-at-home dad for our two kids for six months, then put my résumé together and ease into a job several weeks after starting my search. With my extensive experience in military and civilian logistics and force management, it wouldn't take much effort for a guy like me to land a job offer.*

Well, as you might've guessed, things didn't go as planned. Call me naïve, overly optimistic, or out of touch with the economy. Whatever it was, I was wrong.

Six months after leaving the military, I started my job search. My regrets quickly set in:

---

2 Expiration, term of service

- I hadn't taken advantage of the employment assistance programs offered by the Army and numerous service organizations. I figured I'd been there, done that.

- I hadn't contacted a single recruiter for assistance.

- I hadn't even picked up a book to research job search strategies, despite having been out of the job market for thirty years.

These regrets weighed me down for a long time. But nothing hit me as hard as the realization that I had no idea what I truly wanted to do. Before leaving the military, I had never taken the time to think about what kind of position would fulfill me personally and professionally. I hadn't thought about what I could offer a civilian employer or how I could express my value in terms a civilian would understand. I didn't know myself or my worth like I thought I did.

I struggled with putting my résumé together. It took me more than a month of writing and rewriting to demilitarize my résumé to a point where the average civilian employer would understand what I did in the Army. Once I had my résumé right (or at least what I thought was right at the time), I started doing all the things "they" (you know who "they" are) said you should do: I posted my résumé on popular job sites, applied for jobs online, set up online profiles on social networking sites, and started making connections.

This was about the time I first met Russ Hovendick, author of *How to Interview: What Employers Want to Hear in Today's Competitive Job Market* and *How to Get a Raise: The Correct Way to Ask for an Increase in Salary and Wages.*

At this point, I had applied for about thirty positions, received two phone calls, and zero face-to-face interviews. My first conversation with Russ lasted almost an hour. This is how it started:

"So what do you want to do?" he asked.

"I don't really know," I replied. My answer probably surprised me more than it did him. I realized that the only thing I was sure about was what I *didn't* want. During my time off, I had decided that I didn't want a fifty-to-sixty-hour workweek with long commutes. I didn't want a rigid schedule that required me to be at the office at 0800 sharp. I wanted flexibility on hours, days, and even location.

Unfortunately with my background, I discovered that finding a job or second career that fit my ideal scenario would be tough. I felt that all my experience and training pointed me toward senior manager, director, or similar job titles that would inevitably result in fifty-to-sixty-hour workweeks, long commutes, and strict schedules.

After several conversations with Russ, I spent the next three months preparing and searching. My perspective changed dramatically. I realized that the civilian sector (unless you pursue a defense contractor position) is an unmarked minefield. Civilian employers who have no military background speak a different language. They have different customs and etiquette. Their environment is 180 degrees from military service.

Adjusting to those differences is not unlike deploying to a foreign country—except in the military, we had references, interpreters, intelligence, and yes, were heavily armed.

Unlike many books I've seen on résumé writing, interviewing, and networking, Russ has made the extraordinary leap of asking veterans to know the enemy and know themselves. It reminds me of the timeless quote from General Sun Tzu:

If you know your enemies and know yourself, you will not be imperiled in a hundred battles.

If you do not know your enemies but do know yourself, you will win one and lose one.

If you do not know your enemies nor yourself, you will be imperiled in every single battle.

I'm not saying that hiring managers are "the enemy"—and neither are recruiters like Russ—but you have to be prepared. In this book, he poses a challenge to you transitioning military veterans out there: to know yourself and your "enemy."

In my case, the enemy was me. I knew what I *didn't* want, but not exactly what I *did want* or how to get there.

So I decided to do the FAAB+ exercise in this book, which is a step-by-step worksheet to get you to identify what you have to offer. It wasn't easy at first. I don't know anyone that is military (active, reserve, retired) that isn't somewhat humble. In my case, I had a hard time talking about and putting my accomplishments in writing.

Eventually, I got tired of analyzing whether or not something was too inconsequential or nothing more than routine to add to my worksheet. When I forced myself to be honest, writing down my accomplishments, attributes, and all I had to offer became easy.

If you think about it, we consider so many military demands—like overtime, relocating, and personal sacrifice—to be "part of the job." And when you really get down to it, that commitment is exactly what makes us exceptional candidates for any employer. Let's face it: civilians expect extra pay or time off for meeting requirements like the ones I mentioned.

Bottom line: *never* underestimate your military experience. Yes, our time in the military has made us a different breed of employee. Use that experience to give yourself a competitive edge over the scores of other applicants who have never come close to your level of responsibility.

Not one veteran I know would enter the area of operations without intelligence and air support backing them up. Let this book be your intelligence source, reference, interpreter, patrol bag, and on-call air support rolled into one. Take full advantage of the sample questions, worksheets, anecdotes, and examples. They're tailor-made for ex-service members like you and me. The time to put these tools to use is now.

I am personally putting this book to the test in my job search. And I hope you do the same.

I wish you all the best.

David F. Smith
Colonel, U.S. Army (Retired)

INTRODUCTION

The Employment Conundrum for Ex-Military

The modern American ex-service member returns to civilian life with a new mission: finding a job in the toughest economy since the Great Depression. More than 200,000 military veterans end their service every year and struggle to find employment. In the next ten years, those figures will increase as a result of a half-trillion dollar cut in projected defense spending. U.S. ground forces will be cut by 100,000 troops over the next decade. And with every new jobs report, the rising unemployment rate among military veterans paints an ever bleaker picture. We are in a crisis.

That is why I wrote this book. I've been an executive recruiter for more than twenty years. Every day, I coach job seekers on effective strategies to landing employment. As I began to recruit military servicemen and women and present them to prospective employers, I realized that military job seekers are facing more of an uphill battle than their civilian counterparts.

Consider this: the typical member of the armed forces may have started their military career right out of high school or college and had a branch manager (or, as some call it, "the manpower guy") in Washington, DC managing their entire career. They've never had to draft a résumé, search through job listings, interview for jobs, or face rejection time and again. For many servicemen and women in transition, the civilian workforce might seem an impossible nut to crack.

Civilian employers' preconceived notions about ex-military people don't make it any easier. I'm not naming names here, of course, but here are some common concerns I've heard from managers about hiring service members transitioning out of the military:

- *Why would I hire a military person to supervise here? In the military, their people had to do what they were ordered to do or face a court martial. It doesn't work that way here.*
- *Why would I hire a military person to lead my team? These people come from a highly regimented environment and have never had to think creatively.*
- *Why would I hire a retired military person for my plant? I need someone with youthful energy and drive—not someone at the sunset of their career.*
- *Why would I hire a military person to join my team? They are like government workers. They justify their existence with numbers and technical jargon. I need an action person.*
- *Why would I hire someone who was a commanding officer in the military? I'm looking for a team player, not someone who shouts orders and expects people to obey.*
- *With unemployment at over 7 percent, why would I risk my investment on an unproven commodity?*
- *Why would I hire an Army reservist or a state National Guardsman? Just when you need them most, they'll get called up for service. Then what?*

- *Why would I hire a retired military person? They have guaranteed income, so they won't put forth the effort I need. This job will just be income padding for them.*

- *Why would I hire a military person? We don't even speak the same language. They use all those acronyms and statements about the mission. Just give me someone I can relate to.*

Obviously, there is a huge disconnect between employers and transitioning military service members. Employers aren't seeing the tremendous value that ex-military personnel can offer their organizations. And on the other hand, those ex-military job seekers aren't effectively showing their value. They're not speaking the same language. We need to bridge that gap. And that's what I intend this book to do.

I don't come from a military background, and I don't claim to be an expert on transitioning from military to civilian life. However, as a recruiter who has learned something new every single day for the last twenty years about what employers are looking for, I've picked up some valuable advice that can help you.

Recruiting through my company Client Staffing Solutions in South Dakota, I receive several hundred résumés every week from veterans seeking employment in the civilian sector. I speak with those that show the most promise, learn what they can offer employers, and coach them. If I believe their skills and background would benefit my Fortune 500 food and beverage industry clients, I then arrange job interviews.

I enjoy working with job seekers one-on-one, and I truly believe my life's purpose is to help people take control of their careers. When I began to come across more ex-military personnel searching for jobs a couple of years ago, I realized I needed to tailor my advice to address their needs. I also realized it was impossible to reach the hundreds of thousands of people transitioning out of the armed forces every year to share my knowledge. So I decided to write this book to share everything I know to help our military veterans land the great jobs they deserve. *Deployment to Employment* is the third in a series of career development books by Directional Motivation.

As I say in all my books, ***the little steps you take today will determine your future success.*** Despite the difficult times we live in, I firmly believe that those who take charge of their careers will succeed.

If you're a military veteran, you've undergone rigorous training to accomplish seemingly impossible missions. The job search may feel unnerving, but don't ever forget this: you're part of an elite group of people who can handle anything life throws at you. I offer this guide to you as your strategy source. If you adopt the principles in this book and apply the discipline you learned in the military, there is no reason why you should not succeed.

CHAPTER 1

Starting Over and Recognizing Your Value

Before I go over the winning strategies to getting the job you want, let's get you into a mindset that will allow you to be focused, passionate, and productive. Okay, so the skeptic inside you might be thinking that I don't understand you because I've never spent time in the military. But after twenty years as a recruiter and spending an extensive amount of time mentoring ex-military personnel on how to find employment, I know what you're going through. No matter what I tell you in this book, none of my advice will make any difference unless you approach the information with an open mind and an open heart.

John Kriesel, a former staff sergeant in the Minnesota Army National guard who lost both legs in a roadside bombing in Iraq, is one of the many ex-military men I interviewed for this book. He recalled how he and many of those in his unit had a difficult time finding work in the civilian sector and considered possibly going back to school. Other former soldiers echoed his sentiments and explained that adjusting to civilian life was emotionally devastating. They had grown so accustomed to following orders that they didn't know what to do with their newfound freedom.

"It's almost like being lost," Kriesel told me.

Despondent veterans who've been repeatedly rejected by prospective employers make statements like, "Who's going to want me now?" or "I've already given everything to my country." So, when heavyhearted veterans contact me, I do understand where they're coming from.

If you feel lost, I empathize. But more importantly, I want to snap you out of it! Let this be your wake-up call. A downtrodden, defeatist mentality will repel employers. Despite your best efforts, it will drag you down.

I'm no psychologist, but I know that transitioning to life after the military is essentially starting over. You've recently left a heavily regimented environment where decisions such as what to wear, what time to wake up, what to eat, and how to spend your day are made for you. You may be adjusting to living with your family again or learning how to manage your finances. You may even be dealing with post-traumatic stress disorder or healing from war injuries.

Starting over is certainly not easy for most people leaving the service. Acknowledge that and give yourself permission to take care of yourself first. The job search demands an incredible amount of focus, persistence, and resilience. You'll have highs and lows, so I want to make sure you're fully equipped to handle the emotional rollercoaster.

I tell all of my clients that their overall health and frame of mind are vital to a fruitful job search, but this is especially important for you. I applaud you for taking the first step to getting your life in order. However, you must address your personal needs first in order to present your best self—the real you—to potential employers. As John Kriesel advised, "You've got to make sure that your mind is right and your body is right before you can take these next steps."

Your Secret Weapon: Knowing Your Worth

The biggest, most challenging hurdle that unsuccessful job applicants face is quite often themselves. They do everything they've heard they're supposed to do (i.e., submit résumés and cover letters, answer interview questions, follow up), but somehow they are not winning over employers. Sure, they could blame the economy, the highly competitive industries, or their own lack of qualifications. However, I believe the root cause of the widespread rejection is that **these job seekers fail to recognize their own value.**

Let me explain. In my line of work, I meet thousands of people looking for work. I get to know them by talking on the phone and inquiring about their skills and professional backgrounds. All too often, the start of a conversation with a veteran from the lower ranks goes something like this:

Recruiter: *Tell me about yourself. What did you do in the service?*

Job seeker: *Well, I know you won't be able to help me. I didn't lead anybody.*

From the very start of the conversation, I sense they are shutting down and giving up. They assume that I'm exclusively looking for leadership experience, and their first instinct is to apologize for lacking the experience I'm supposedly looking for. It's as if they don't believe they *deserve* a good job.

In reality, I look for candidates with a strong sense of personal accountability, people who strive to function at their highest—no matter what positions they've held. The most successful candidates I've placed with my corporate clients were those that took on every job responsibility as a personal mission. I know what my corporate clients want out of their employees, so that's what I deliver.

People coming out of the military are especially guilty of failing to recognize their value. They tend to equate their worth with their specific job duties without considering their contributions from a broader perspective. Nolan Ruby, Directional Motivation's veterans affairs advisor, served in the U.S. Marine Corps. He remembers joking around with his fellow Marines that when they left the service, they would either become janitors or security guards because that's all they felt qualified to do.

I hear this from many ex-military job seekers, particularly those in the lower ranks who did not have people reporting to them. Here's another common example: a driver will typically say, "I was just a driver. The most important thing I did was deliver stuff from one place to another." I cringe whenever I hear job applicants minimize their roles like this. So much valuable experience goes to waste when you make statements like that. Honestly, do you really think your role defending the United States can be compared to a taxi driver or a pizza delivery person? Of course not!

If you were a driver for the armed forces, you did more than drive vehicles. You solved problems through maintenance checks and prevented transport crises by making sure the vehicle was operating at its best. You were responsible for moving millions of dollars of equipment from one danger zone to another. You might have been in charge of transporting very important officials like the Secretary of State. Do you think your superiors would have assigned those heavy-duty responsibilities to any old driver?

My guess is that your units considered you the ultimate authority over the vehicles you drove and maintained. Instead of going to a 300-page reference manual when they had questions about operating the vehicle, the members of your unit came to you. Most likely, no one ever questioned whether your vehicle was ready to go because you had proven time and again that you were religious about keeping it in top working order. Your unit had the utmost confidence that your vehicle was prepared to enter a danger zone at a moment's notice.

And yet, there are many ex-military drivers out there going to job interviews and telling hiring managers that all they did was "drive a truck" or were "just a mechanic." If you fit the description above, then your job responsibilities were a personal crusade. You knew your vehicle intimately and that exemplified your passion and work ethic, which exceeds the norm in the civilian world.

But how would a civilian hiring manager know this if you didn't explain it? How could they? Only you can make them understand. And before you can do that, you must know it and understand it yourself. Quite simply, you must believe in yourself. You cannot hope to convince an employer that you would make a valuable addition to their team if you don't believe it yourself.

Start by thinking of your previous roles from the 200,000-foot level. How would a mission be compromised if your unit didn't have you, the private E-2, the seaman recruit, the airman first class? What operation would have been delayed if you hadn't transported a shipment on schedule? How many people's lives would have been at risk if you hadn't done your routine engine check on the aircraft? You may have heard about another unit whose mission was hindered because one person failed to do an assignment.

Now think of the tasks you did in order to raise your level of preparedness and avoid the mistakes that others had made. Did members of your unit ever compliment you on your abilities? Did they ever make statements about why you were better in your role than others? These statements are valuable as you begin to understand what you have to offer employers.

* *

Action Item: FAAB+ Sheet

When you hear the word "fab," you might think it's a shortcut for "fabulous." However, FAB sheets list a person's features, accomplishments, and benefits. Recruiters typically have job candidates fill these out. The traditional template uses three columns. However, you are more than the "typical" job seeker. We at Directional Motivation always strive to push our audience to get the most out of our products. In this book, I've supercharged the old template into my own version I call FAAB+, which stands for features, accomplishments, attributes, benefits, plus.

This is one of the most effective exercises in this book. Whenever I work with job seekers who need that extra boost, I always have them do this exercise. It leads to phenomenal results, so I'm making this a requirement for you. This activity will help you flesh out information and give you a burst of confidence. It will also serve as an aid for writing your résumé and preparing for job interviews.

Before we go through each part of the acronym, I suggest you download the FAAB+ Sheet template from www.directionalmotivation.com.[3] The website also features a webinar explaining this exercise.

Features

These are the cut-and-dried facts about you that are most likely in your résumé or military file. Dedicate one row in the chart for each position you held in the military and write down your job responsibilities. Write down every single task, no matter how small. Part of recognizing your value is being able to identify how you spent your time in previous jobs. Avoid technical jargon and be direct, simple, and concise. If you get stuck, imagine yourself explaining your typical day in the military to your ten-year-old cousin.

---

3 From the Resources tab, you'll see the link to Worksheets.

Accomplishments

For each position in your features column, list your successes and how you achieved them. You already listed the tasks that you performed in the features column. Every little task inched you closer toward something. If you reached those goals, list them here. If you came close to your goals, go ahead and list how close you came.

Don't judge yourself or dismiss your accomplishments as being merely "part of the job." Small victories are meaningful and every unit needs them to survive. After you list your accomplishments, you may realize that you left out the features that led to those accomplishments. Go back and add those to the features column. Notice how the features relate to the accomplishments.

Here are some examples of military accomplishments to get you going:

- named squad leader in first week of basic training
- moved up to NCO[4] ranks after two years
- resolved major logistics errors
- completed extra electronics coursework during ROTC
- created a new SOP[5] for community outreach that was implemented by the entire command
- assisted in editing new counterinsurgency regulation
- served as a recorder for judicial hearing board
- received Airman of the Year award

---

4 non-commissioned officer

5 standard operating procedure

- planned multiple retirement, deployment, and change-of-command ceremonies
- briefed members of Congress
- served as escort for government officials visiting the base

There should be at least twenty items on this list. In fact, think about both your personal and professional accomplishments. If you're having a difficult time, here are some areas to consider:

- Did you work while attending school?
- Have you supervised others? Ask them for their honest opinions about your performance and how you impacted their lives.
- Has your commanding officer ever recognized you formally or informally for a job well done?
- What kinds of awards have you won?
- How have you influenced members of your unit?
- How have you influenced your unit as a whole?
- Have you ever done volunteer work? What did you contribute?
- What have you failed at? What did you learn from those failures and how did they change you?
- Have you ever faced an obstacle that seemed impossible to get through?
- How have you made a difference in someone else's life?
- Have you ever created something from nothing?

- Have you ever faced a fear?
- Have you ever stood up to injustice?
- Have you ever changed the status quo? How?

Attributes

Review both columns of each row you've completed so far and write the qualities you demonstrated in each row. Your attributes are your strengths. Regardless of position, industry, or employer you have, you carry these attributes with you. For example, if your accomplishment was "named expert rifleman in basic training," you might write in the attributes column, "persistent, passionate, accurate."

Benefits

This column requires you to push yourself by thinking from your superior's perspective. Typically, I tell job seekers to list how their accomplishments and attributes benefitted their employer. In your case, you can list how your accomplishments benefitted your base, station, or ship. This is the turning point of this exercise because it will naturally lend itself to the next column.

Plus (+)

This last column will take your A-game to the next level. However, I recommend holding off on completing this column until you read Chapter 4. Don't worry, I won't let you forget about this very important column. I have included a reminder in that chapter for you.

In the + column, you take the ideas from the benefits column and translate that into to how you can specifically benefit the company where you hope to work. In other words, you've shown what you did for your previous employers. Now show what you can do for this new employer. The only way to effectively complete this column is by researching the company you are applying to.

To see a couple of FAAB+ sample entries, go to pages 69-70.

* *

Regardless of what rank you held in the military, I know for a fact that you have something valuable to offer employers. Despite the high unemployment rate for veterans (9.9 percent in 2012),[6] there are literally hundreds of companies that need your knowledge, skills, and experience in order to operate more efficiently and increase profits.

I know this because I talk to these employers every day. There is a high demand for you out there in the civilian world. As president of a staffing agency, I specialize in placing job seekers in the food and beverage manufacturing industry. Most veterans have never had experience in this industry, but I've known many who have successfully demonstrated to employers that their skills were useful to that industry.

Countless hiring managers have told me that people from the armed forces are high performers for many reasons:

- They're problem solvers.
- They're inherently hands-on.
- They work well in teams.
- Managers don't have to "babysit" them because they're self-disciplined and work independently.
- They learn quickly.

6 "Employment Situation of Veterans Summary," released March 20, 2013, U.S. Department of Labor, Bureau of Labor Statistics, accessed April 4, 2013, http://www.bls.gov/news.release/vet.nr0.htm.

- They excel in diverse environments, including rough industrial settings.
- They're task-oriented and have a strong sense of accountability for every aspect of their job.

Do you have these valuable attributes? If yes, then congratulations! These are the kinds of qualities employers are looking for.

It always amazes me when an employer explains to me that their company's food manufacturing plant is refrigerated and then asks if my ex-military candidate would be able to handle such harsh conditions. These employers are merely being conscientious, but their comments reveal how little they know about military life.

Think about it. If you've been in combat, you've had to work in tougher conditions than most people could ever fathom. You've trudged through mud, fought off camel spiders, contended with snakes, hidden in desert caves, endured extreme cold, and thirsted through baking heat. You've survived violent gun battles and saved the lives of your fellow soldiers.

When you contrast your previous work environment to a cramped office or a soot-filled manufacturing plant, don't you feel like you can excel in virtually any environment? Compare the worst possible mistake you can make in a corporate setting to the worst possible mistake you could make on a mission for the U.S. Armed Forces. Consider what you've had to accomplish in eight hours on a military mission versus what you'd be expected to accomplish in an eight-hour shift at a civilian job. If you don't believe you can bring tremendous value to a civilian employer, you should.

One of the ex-military men I interviewed for this book was Aaron Curtis, who served more than twenty years in the Army. In the summer of 2012, after two and a half months of searching for a job, he was offered a position in Washington State as the senior quality engineer for a German aerospace company. Aaron always tells his old comrades, many still in Afghanistan, "You already possess the skills to be successful." He reminds them that the job search may feel foreign, but hey, that's nothing new. They've already been overseas. They know what it's like to navigate through foreign territory. I encourage you to consider the job search as "foreign territory" to explore, understand, and benefit from.

Civilian employers may not understand the level of responsibility required of every military position and, therefore, may not comprehend the value you would bring if they brought you onboard. It's your responsibility to explain it to them. I'll go into more detail about explaining those responsibilities in Chapter 4. But for now, the FAAB+ exercise hopefully got you pumped up about being you. If you truly believe in yourself and persist in moving toward your goals, you'll be just fine.

CHAPTER 2

Adjusting Your Mindset to the Civilian World

The civilian world is messy. It's chaotic, political, and many things are subject to unexpected change. The civilian world is full of a wide variety of personalities and emotions. Learning to establish yourself as a professional in the civilian world will require some acclimation. This chapter gives you four specific strategies to put yourself in the best possible frame of mind for your job search.

Steer Clear of the Entitlement Mentality

This is not an easy subject to talk about, but since I do intend this book to be a wake-up call to veterans seeking employment, the message is extremely important. **Your military service does not entitle you to a job.** Companies are looking for employees who will contribute value and help them increase profitability, enhance customer loyalty, decrease costs, implement greater efficiency, and more. They are seeking high performers.

I mean absolutely no disrespect here, and I sincerely appreciate your service to our country, but **employers don't *owe* you a job.** Every now and then, I meet an ex-service member looking for a job, carrying around that entitlement mentality. They give off the impression that they've already proven themselves and should not need to do it again. In their minds, they shouldn't have to start at the bottom of a company or industry. They're hell-bent on the notion that employers should hire them solely because they defended this country.

This mentality will ruin your chances of finding employment. If I can sense the sour attitude from a phone call, imagine how it would come off in person during a job interview.

As John Kriesel pointed out in our conversation, our society has come a long way from the cold reception the Vietnam War veterans faced when they returned home. With the strong "Support Our Troops" sentiment, it's easy to fall in the mindset of entitlement. But let me tell you, that attitude repels employers. It sends the message: *I don't care what you think of me. I don't have to fit in. I don't have to know how to deal with people or work in a team. I don't have to prove myself to you or anyone. You ought to hire me to show your appreciation for my service.*

If you approach the job search feeling entitled, it will be obvious in the way you carry yourself and communicate with prospective employers. You'll be viewed as an undesirable candidate with a chip on your shoulder. It's an ugly impression, and one that might foster a detrimental and erroneous conception of the military in general. What a shame.

Study Your Superiors

Sometimes, people tend to have tunnel vision and focus only on what they are doing in the moment. However, that perspective is very limiting, particularly if you are getting ready to transition to another field. If you are currently in military service, you still have an opportunity to learn from the people who lead your unit.

Take note of the decisions they make and the factors that go into their decision-making process. Watch how your superiors handle discord within the lower ranks, manage relationships with their peers, and prioritize multiple missions. Study how they respond to unexpected situations and crises. Imagine yourself in their shoes in similar situations.

Don't be shy. Talk to them and glean whatever knowledge you can while you have easy access to them. You will discover that their experiences can offer valuable lessons that apply equally well in the civilian world.

Learn How to Ask for Help

Self-sufficiency can be a good thing, but it can be detrimental at times. I've heard from many ex-service members that military culture ingrains a belief that each person is in charge of their own career. There's a sense that asking for help shows weakness, lack of capability, even failure.

I get it. You don't want pity. You can take care of yourself, and it's nobody's business what you're going through, right? You may even wear this attitude like a badge of honor. However, I guarantee that the job search will be significantly easier, shorter, and have exponentially higher chances of success if you ask for help.

Don't get me wrong. You are, indeed, the driving force behind your job search. Your initiative will determine the outcome. But that initiative includes reaching out to those that make a difference for you. You're doing the legwork, research, soul searching, networking, marketing, selling, and follow-up. But there are myriad resources out there that can help you maximize your efforts. I've listed some in the Appendix, but I'm sure there are many others available.

Take advantage of military programs like the Veterans Retraining Assistance Program (VRAP), Army Career and Alumni Program (ACAP), and Employer Partnership of the Armed Forces. Seek mentors and career counselors. Talk to your military chaplain. Reach out to your colleagues. Ask friends and family members to introduce you to any potential connections in your desired industry.

The old adage, "You are the company you keep" is very true. Surround yourself with positive people and learn from them. This is especially important when seeking a mentor. You may not have the luxury of being able to cherry-pick a mentor, but here are some qualities to look for:

- has a track record of success
- has a circle of influence
- faced adversity and overcame it
- will be honest with you (sometimes brutally honest, if needed!)

Aaron Curtis, the former Army officer I introduced in the previous chapter, worked with a mentor from the nonprofit American Corporate Partners. The organization pairs executives and higher-ups in the corporate world one-on-one with veterans seeking employment at no cost. In the organization's latest report, 1,500 veterans were working with mentors on résumé building, networking, leadership, and job market knowledge. The organization also offers a free online Quick Question Community that allows current and ex-military job seekers and their immediate family members to ask experienced business leaders questions about employment, career development, and small business.

Aaron's mentor is an upper level manager at General Mills. "The fact that he's there to answer my calls and weird questions—that's invaluable to me," Curtis said. "It lets me know that there's someone there for me."

Industry recruiters have a special role in the job search, too. (I promise this is not a shameless plug for my staffing agency.) No matter what recruiting agency you go with, any good recruiter will have established relationships with employers. They earn a commission every time they place a candidate in a position, so your success is in their best interest as well. They'll advise you on how to craft your résumé, help you prepare for interviews, and hopefully give you insider information on the company's culture not found in the job listings.

Remember, your relationship with recruiters is a two-way street. When they send you to an interview, they are vouching for you as a serious, credible job applicant. They've spent years building relationships with those corporate clients and are putting their reputation on the line because they believe you'd be a good fit. I highly encourage you to follow their advice.

If you've gone through basic training, you've done the forty-foot, five-level skyscraper exercise. Think back to that training. In teams of four, you climbed to the top with no one to help you but each other. That's an exercise in trust. You would've found it difficult and dangerous to climb that skyscraper alone, right? Well, the difficulties of job hunting are of a different nature, but you need not face them alone either. Consider your chaplain, career counselor, mentor, and recruiter as members of your new unit—your civilian unit. Rely on them just as you once relied on your comrades. When you feel hesitant to depend on others, think back to that skyscraper exercise and trust that no one on your team will let you fall.

Be Open to Building Relationships with Civilians

It's natural for you to feel as though the only people you can connect with are those who once served in the military. Civilians cannot fully grasp what you've experienced in the military because they haven't walked in your boots. I've read multiple books about military life and interviewed many ex-service members in the making of this book and still, I can never fully understand what you've experienced.

That was one of the biggest lessons for Brian Cudmore, who spent four years in the Marine Corps and now works as a hospital staffer in Oregon. Military people need to realize that they're going to have to form some bond with people who have no idea what they've gone through," he said. "That's a really hard thing."

It took some time for Brian to stop comparing the way people from the military did certain things versus how civilians did them. He eventually came to realize that it wasn't necessary for someone to be like him—in other words, ex-military—to be a good friend, coworker, or boss. If your goal is to maximize your chances for a successful job search in the civilian world, you'll need to make meaningful connections with people—especially civilians.

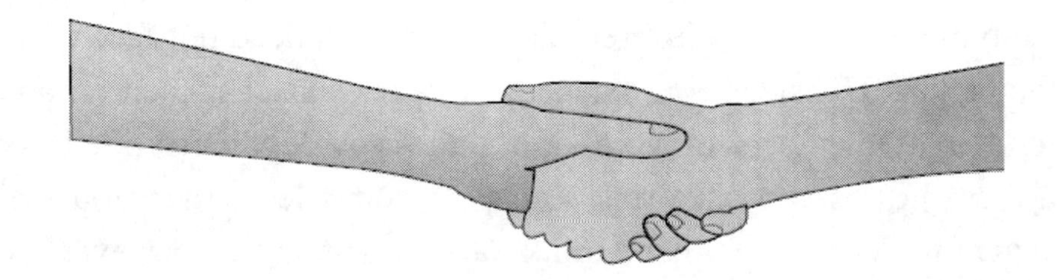

Tap into your existing networks and expand them by meeting people. Attend networking events, rotary club meetings, industry conferences, trade association get-togethers, and job fairs to meet quality people in person. The more people who know that you are looking for a job, the greater the chances you'll have to make valuable connections.

Of the many ex-military folks I interviewed who found good jobs, all of them credited their success to their connections with others. In fact, according to experts quoted in an article from the *Wall Street Journal*, "the single best method of getting a job remains a referral from a company employee."[7]

A word of caution here: desperation is a turnoff. When you're out meeting people, your primary goal is get to know them—not to ask for work. It's perfectly acceptable to let them know you're transitioning out of the military and looking for work, but keep in mind that networking is all about building relationships. When other people get to know, like, and trust you—as the old marketing principle goes—you'll open yourself up to more opportunities.

****

Action Items:

1) Do research and compile a list of organizations in your community, including trade associations, civic associations, social groups, and community groups. The more tailored you can make your search to get to your desired industry or position, the better. However, keep an open mind. You never know what contacts might prove valuable.

---

7 Lauren Weber, "Your Résumé vs. Oblivion: Inundated Companies Resort to Software to Sift Job Applications for Right Skills," *Wall Street Journal*, January 24, 2012, http://online.wsj.com/article/SB10001424052970204624204577178941034941330.html.

2) Join virtual communities. Go online and see what kind of virtual communities would help you make connections in your desired field. If you haven't already, set up profiles on Meetup, LinkedIn, and Facebook. Explore the sites and find networking opportunities within the next two weeks. I am, by no means, an expert in social media, but I know how powerful these outlets can be.

Here are a few of my quick tips on the main social networks:

- Meetup is an incredibly valuable website to find local gatherings of people that have similar interests. Depending on your area, you can find meetups on almost any interest, including business networking, fitness, parenting, travel, etc.

- Use LinkedIn to find groups in your interest area and join the discussions posted on the group page. LinkedIn is also a great place to find job fairs, networking events, and job listings. In fact, if you're not familiar with using LinkedIn, check out Directional Motivation's free in-depth training webinar available at www.directionalmotivation.com.[8]

- Facebook has a group feature and event feature similar to those on Meetup and LinkedIn.

3) Research events happening within a fifty-mile radius within the next month, figure out logistics, and put them on your calendar. There are plenty of places online to find career fairs for military veterans, including virtual events that allow you to attend from the comfort of your own home. Here are just a few:

- http://roa.corporategrayonline.com/jobfairs

- https://events.recruitmilitary.com/

---

8 To get to the LinkedIn webinar, go to the Military tab and click on Internet Researching Tips.

- http://www.military.com/career-expo/career-fair-calendar-2013/
- http://vetjobs.com/media/upcoming-military-related-career-fairs/

4) Get business cards. If you have the good fortune of meeting someone who can help you land a job—or someone who can introduce you to the right people—you need more than your charming personality to remain memorable to the other person. You need professionally printed business cards with your contact information. Imagine having a great conversation with someone and you both agree to keep in touch. Then you realize the best you can do is to handwrite your name and number on a napkin. It doesn't sound very professional, does it?

If you need help designing your card, visit your local print shop or search for a graphic designer. However, there are so many places on the Internet to order inexpensive, high-quality business cards, I recommend checking online first. Lifehacker, a website about software and personal productivity tools, names the following as the best business card printing sites[9]:

- Moo.com
- GotPrint.com
- VistaPrint.com
- JukeBoxPrint.com
- OvernightPrints.com

---

9 Alan Henry, "Five Best Business Card Printing Sites," Lifehacker.com, accessed June 5, 2013, http://lifehacker.com/5973319/five-best-business-card-printing-sites.

Now let's discuss what information to include on your business card. At minimum, you should include your name, phone number, and e-mail address. If you've set up your LinkedIn profile and you feel good about it, put the customized LinkedIn public profile URL on your card. (By customized, I mean your name should be in the URL rather than a string of random letters.)

To step it up a notch—which is what Directional Motivation is all about—I recommend adding your value statement. This is a concise statement about you and what you have to offer. Value statements are used in many ways. Small business owners might use them when promoting their businesses. Corporations might feature them in their taglines or on their websites. Much has been written about value statements, but my favorite description comes from the *For Dummies* book series: "your value statement should help you establish instant credibility, curiosity, and likeability."[10]

Crafting your value statement does not have to be a tedious process. It doesn't have to be fancy or clever. Think simple and direct. Remember, you'll have very limited space on your business card, so the statement must be short. You may even consider the possibility of placing it on the backside of your card, depending on the length of the statement and card's design.

To give you some ideas and show you how easy it can be to craft your value statement, here are a few examples I drafted after researching various positions in the military:

- For a Navy steelworker: *Skilled steelworker with precision and vision.*

---

10 Joshua Waldman, "Put Together Your Value Statement to Use in Your Job Search," from *Job Searching with Social Media For Dummies*, http://www.dummies.com/how-to/content/put-together-your-value-statement-to-use-in-your-j.html.

- For someone in Air Force Pararescue: *Rescue and recovery specialist. I handle emergencies and teach others how do it.*

- For a U.S. Coast Guard Operations Specialist: *Expert researcher and planner with extensive technical experience operating satellite communications, global positions navigation, and identification systems.*

And my last tip on business cards: Keep some with you at all times. Carry them in your wallet and stash some in your car. You never know when you'll meet a valuable contact.

****

There are so many opportunities to meet new people. The secret is to stay active and open to new opportunities. Go ahead, step out of your comfort zone and mix with civilians. (We're not so bad, I promise!) You'll also likely meet other military veterans who've gone through the same employment search and will be happy to offer tips.

Make friends and learn what they have to offer. These social skills will help you no matter what industry you're looking to break into. Your ability to connect with people will be obvious when you're out networking, attending job fairs, meeting with recruiters and career counselors, and interviewing with employers.

CHAPTER 3
Find Where You Fit

I heard a poignant story from Jonathan Anderson, an Army chaplain based out of Ohio. He told me about a conversation he had with a talented individual from his group struggling to find employment as he approached his end date. "All I want is a job that pays money," the fellow said. "If I didn't want the job, I wouldn't apply for it."

Let's think about this: A job that pays money. If only the world were so simple. His story reminds me of the hundreds of ex-military job hunters who contact me unwilling to say much beyond "What do you got?" In those instances, I ask them to tell me about themselves so I can determine which of my client companies would benefit from their skills, experience, and personality.

Military life has a starkly different approach to job placement. In the Army, they look for slots to fill or as my friend, retired Army officer Tim Mariner describes it, "a hole to plug." Your branch manager or "manpower guy" in Washington, DC places you based on your military classification and the military's need at that time.

As you know, if you're an E-6 in the Army with an MOS[11] of 42 (human resources), then you're automatically eligible to fill any open E-6 slot in human resources. If you're about to graduate from the Naval Academy hoping to be an engineer for the Navy, but the

11 military occupational skill

Navy has a shortage of intelligence officers, there's a high probability you'll have to be an intelligence officer.

Typically, you wouldn't be required to talk with an interviewer who would assess whether or not your personality, work habits, and leadership style fit in a certain group. Based on my conversations with ex-military personnel, the career manager may not necessarily factor in unique qualities such as your character traits, passion, or potential the way a civilian recruiter or hiring manager would. In the civilian world, companies have different cultures, management styles, goals, values, and work environments. My job as a recruiter is to help job seekers find employment in positions and companies where they fit well. Recruiters are like matchmakers. We're looking for just the right chemistry that will lead to compatibility from both sides.

So let's go back to Chaplain Anderson's story about the gentleman who wanted a job that paid money. It's not enough to find "a job that pays money." You deserve more than that. Yes, we all need to earn a living to put food on the table. But wouldn't it be great to love what you do for a living? Wouldn't it be great to find something meaningful to you? I encourage you to search for employers that will offer you the opportunity to develop your unique skills, challenge yourself, and grow.

I frequently meet veterans who have no idea what they'd like to do. Chaplain Anderson often counsels Army officers who have been told what they were going to do next throughout their entire careers. They tell him, "I've never had to think about it before." So instead of facing this head-on, many shy away from introspection and simply hope things will work out. Other people, Chaplain Anderson said, admit they've been in a military job for so long that they've grown tired of it, but are afraid to try something else. They don't want to risk the chance of failure.

In a bizarre way, the feeling is similar to the prison inmate who has been incarcerated for twenty years. While behind bars, all he can think about is what he would do if he were free—only to find that when that day finally arrives, he's paralyzed. For the first time in a long time, there's no prison guard walking behind him, watching his every move. There's no set time for showering, eating, or going outdoors. Now he must not only make minor day-to-day choices, but big decisions that will impact the rest of his life. If he has a family, his decisions will impact them, too. He must teach himself how to live as a free man. With only pennies in his pocket, he wonders how he's going to earn a living.

Of course, I mean no disrespect in drawing a parallel between our country's heroes to ex-convicts. I only make the comparison because I counsel people in dire circumstances on a regular basis as a volunteer prison chaplain. I completely understand the feeling of not knowing what to do with newfound freedom.

After leaving the highly regimented military life, it's up to you to take charge and keep yourself disciplined to land the job you want. Now comes the million dollar question: What *do* you want?

Job seeker and retired Army Colonel David Smith from Georgia said, "My biggest frustration, to be honest, is not that there are no jobs. It's that I don't know 100 percent what I want to do."

After working for thirty years in military and civilian management positions, he had spent several months at home with his two kids, a four-year-old and a nine-year-old. He also discovered a newfound love for golf. After some soul searching, David wasn't sure he wanted to return to the "forty-to-sixty-hour a week bust-your-butt corporate world."

When I caught up with David a week later, he said he would love to be a general manager at a golf course. The problem was he didn't have any professional experience in the golf industry. Unlike his potential competitors for that kind of position, he hadn't held previous positions in service-oriented industries. He'd never worked at a pro shop or been a restaurant manager at a golf course.

Personally, I'm confident David would do an excellent job managing a golf course given his extensive experience in leadership, budgeting, and management. For him, the task ahead is finding a way into the golf industry—even if it's a position a few levels below golf course manager—and then translating his current skill set to the lower position. From there, it's all about gaining the right experience, making valuable connections, and proving himself in the industry. Translating one's military experience into civilian positions is the challenge many ex-service members face and we'll discuss how to do that later in this book. For now, I bring up David's story as an example of someone who took the time to think about what he truly wanted.

I encourage you to do your own soul searching. What are you passionate about? What kind of work would be meaningful for you? What kind of people do you want to associate with? What kind of industry do you want to surround yourself in? Imagine yourself at 100 years old looking back at your life. Would you regret spending so many hours in a job you hated or would you feel grateful to have earned a living doing what you loved?

An old adage says, “It’s better to be at the bottom of a ladder you want to climb than at the top of a ladder you don’t.”

Although many longtime military veterans have spent much of their careers managing people, transitioning into civilian employment often requires them to let go of being the one in charge. I’ve come across many longtime military personnel who insist that “manager” *must* be in their job titles. They may have led people for a majority of their career and are hesitant to get back in the trenches as a team member.

However, flexibility is the key. If you let yourself get hung up on job titles, you limit your opportunities. Rather than obsessing over job *titles*, focus on job *descriptions* that resonate with you. Be open to starting in the lower levels of a company or an industry and then use that experience as a springboard to management positions in the future. Civilian employers will be pleased to hear that you are open to lower level roles like production supervisor, assistant manager, supply management specialist, or sales coordinator. In David’s case, going straight for a golf course manager position without any experience in the golf industry would be tough. So I encouraged him to consider applying to mid-level positions in the golf industry.

Small Company v. Big Company

As you think about your career track and ideal work environment, consider if you would most likely excel at a big Fortune 500 company or a smaller company. To give you a clearer perspective, here’s a quick list of pros and cons of working for big corporations versus working at startups and small and medium-size companies.

Note: these are generalizations based on my experience as a recruiter. There are always exceptions.

Big Corporation Pros:

1) They have big budgets for advertising, marketing, and research and development of new products, which keeps them competitive in the marketplace.
2) They offer excellent training and development programs.
3) Employees have a defined career track.
4) The size of the companies allows employees to focus on one area of development.
5) Big names look great on résumés.
6) They offer benefits and relocation packages.

Big Corporation Cons:

1) Corporate culture can be very exclusive. You must fit the mold to progress within the organization.
2) Employees have limited interaction with top-level executives.
3) Employees have the "small fish in a big pond" feeling.
4) It may be more difficult to make an impact and get noticed.
5) New ideas must be filtered through multiple departments. In other words, things happen slowly.

Startup, Small and Medium-Size Company Pros:

1) Employees interact more frequently with high-level executives.
2) Employees have more diverse responsibilities and exposure to multiple facets of the business.
3) Decisions are made and implemented quickly.
4) Thc companies are more flexible to industry changes.
5) Employees have opportunities to get promoted quickly.

Startup, Small and Medium-Size Company Cons:

1) Resources can be limited for expansion and new product development.
2) Companies are vulnerable to economic pressures and possible buyouts.
3) Career advancement can be quick, but limited due to flat management structure.
4) Benefits may be less.

Think Outside the Box

Often, military veterans will only consider the obvious options for employment. For example, if you're a diesel mechanic, your first inclination might be to search for jobs at major manufacturers such as Caterpillar or Detroit. Of course, I encourage you to shoot for jobs at your ideal companies, but I don't want you to miss out on the sea of opportunities with other possible employers, however unlikely some may seem. There are plenty of companies that could benefit from your skills. For example, a diesel mechanic might never have considered working for a farm equipment dealership, trucking company, or an office complex with a warehouse.

Maybe the other options don't sound as appealing as mega manufacturing companies, but they can provide exceptional opportunities with the potential to work your way up. When I advise veterans to explore alternative options like the ones I mentioned above, many of them are particularly surprised at my recommendation to seek employment with farm equipment dealerships. I happen to know many happily employed people who work at those types of dealerships maintaining equipment. They tell me those jobs offer a great hometown type of work atmosphere in rural family-friendly communities. Without a doubt, your military background as a diesel mechanic would bring tremendous value to these operations.

Think outside the box and explore alternative options. If you don't see yourself in corporate America, consider careers in government, nonprofit organizations, or education. When you finally realize that you have the power to add value no matter where you work, you'll be surprised at the rush of optimism and excitement you'll get.

Let's explore the many possibilities using an example of someone with a background in logistics, supply chain, or platoon leadership. Those skills could easily transfer to companies such as retail distributers, parts manufacturers, retail grocery, and food and beverage manufacturers. In that case, you can add the following well-known companies to your list of prospects: J.C. Penney, Men's Wearhouse, Target, Kohl's, Boeing, FedEx, Kroger, Hy-Vee, Safeway, Smithfield Foods, PepsiCo, and Frito-Lay.

From there, you may want to check the lesser known companies that offer similar products and services such as Foremost Farms USA, Johnsonville Sausage, Snyder's-Lance, Macy's, Dick's Sporting Goods, Enterprise Rent-A-Car, just to name a few. Be open to the possibilities that exist within any organization, regardless of size. And while we're on the subject of companies to research, check out the compilations of military-friendly employers at MilitaryTimes.com and MilitaryFriendly.com.

In fact, let's take thinking outside the box a step further. If you're not qualified for positions that interest you, explore what you need to do to become qualified. What do you need to do? Get certified? Pass a test? Go back to school? Enroll in classes part-time while working? All of these are within your reach.

As veterans, you have access to many government-sponsored programs designed to assist you through your transition. I mentioned a few of these in Chapter 2. However, you may not be aware of private programs, such as the Wings for Heroes scholarship program established by Dr. Mikel Harry, co-creator of a well-known business management certification called Six Sigma. Dr. Harry is a retired Marine Corps officer and philanthropist. I've had a few conversations with him and can tell he's passionate about helping the military community.

The Wings for Heroes scholarship—eligible to active and reservist duty military personnel, transitioning soldiers and veterans, and their immediate family members—pays for 80 percent of the tuition for obtaining Six Sigma Black Belt Certification. Scholarship recipients also get one-on-one coaching online by certified subject matter experts. Depending on the type of position you're looking for, this impressive business management certification could give you the competitive edge you need.[12]

If you're interested in going back to school or taking courses at a university, check out *Military Times*' annual list of best colleges for vets. Maybe you'll find one that (1) offers a program that will ultimately help you get where you want to be in your career, and (2) will give you the support you need. Bellevue University in Nebraska, for example, ranked as one of the top schools for military veterans because it participates in the Yellow Ribbon Program, has a veterans office, and accepts American Council on Education credits. The university also has over 4,000 military-affiliated students, according to the most recent survey.[13]

Think of your job search as another chance. You're starting over a little older and wiser than you were before you joined the military. You know yourself better. Your skills are stronger. And the best part is now you have control over what to do next in your career.

---

12 Six Sigma Wings for Heroes, http://www.ssmimilitaryscholarship.com/.

13 "Best for Vets: Colleges 2013," *Military Times*, November 11, 2012, http://projects.militarytimes.com/jobs/best-for-vets/2013/colleges/4-year/.

* *

Action Item: Find Where You Fit Exercise

Think freely for a moment and get ready to start writing down your thoughts. Nobody is reading over your shoulder. Take a chance and allow yourself to think. Don't edit yourself and do not judge yourself. Let your thoughts and creativity flow without thinking about the "how" for now.

- Answer the following questions:[14]
- What do you enjoy doing?
- If you had one year to live and were paid a decent income no matter what you did, how would you spend your time?
- What would you do if there were no chance you would fail?
- What would you do if it didn't matter what your paycheck was?
- What skills come naturally to you?
- What kind of environment do you thrive in?
- Think back to your military experience. What moments did you feel most alive?
- What training sessions did you feel most comfortable participating in?
- What accomplishments are you most proud of?
- What are some of the most unforgettable experiences you've had in the military?

---

14 You may download the Directional Motivation worksheet called "From Military to Civilian Workplace: Find Where You Fit" from www.directionalmotivation.com and write your answers there.

****

Action Item: Go Online to Figure Out What You Want

Explore the following free online tools (my favorites among many) to help you identify your job hunt goals and overall professional goals:

- For those still exploring the types of positions and industries they are best suited for, I recommend setting up an account at www.wetfeet.com. You can read industry summaries and common jobs in those industries. The information is definitely not in-depth, but it is helpful as a starter.

- Monster Career Snapshots features quick profiles of positions, including job qualifications, rate of growth, and listings for that position currently on Monster. The direct link is http://my.monster.com/Job-Profiles/GetProfile.aspx.

- Once you've decided on the position or multiple positions that interest you, I recommend researching for more in-depth information. Gottamentor.com features a very helpful Career and Occupational Readiness Evaluation, which the site refers to as COREvaluations. This user-friendly tool allows website visitors to see how their experience matches up with specific positions. At the end of the online survey, you'll instantly get a scorecard and action plan.

- And lastly, the Employer Partnership of the Armed Forces has a useful tool on its website called the Military Skills Translator. It allows users to select specific military occupations and see civilian skills that match. Check it out at http://mst.military.com/mst/ep/mos-translator.

* *

A Word of Caution on Starting Businesses and Partnerships

Every now and then, I meet a veteran who simply can't imagine working for someone else. He might have entrepreneurial instincts and even a great business idea. Or maybe he and his best Army buddy are skilled mechanics and they decide to open up a shop together. What could be better than starting a business with the guy that has always had your back? If you've been toying around with the idea of starting your own business, I urge you to be extremely cautious.

Only about half of all new businesses survive five years or more and just one-third of them survive ten years or more, according to the U.S. Small Business Administration.[15] Pretty steep odds, for sure. It's extremely difficult for anyone to establish a small business and rely on it for steady income right away. For transitioning military, it's even more difficult because adjusting back to civilian life alone poses additional hurdles.

Business partnerships have an even more dismal failure rate. It's a commonly held belief within the banking industry that 80 percent, if not higher, of all partnerships fail. Having worked in the banking industry many years ago as a loan representative, I can vouch for that. Banks typically consider partnerships to be very risky, which is why they require substantial collateral on small business loans to partnerships.

Here's my two cents for you aspiring entrepreneurs: take your time and get settled in a stable job before you go full force into your business. At the very least, secure a part-time job in the early stages of your business. Be extra vigilant with startup costs.

---

15 "Frequently Asked Questions about Small Businesses," released September 2012, U.S. Small Business Administration Office of Advocacy, accessed April 15, 2013, http://www.sba.gov/sites/default/files/FAQ_Sept_2012.pdf.

Recently, I spoke with a former Marine who had saved more than $70,000 during his eight years in the Marine Corps. When he left the service, he used all of it to start a business based on an idea he had never researched. If he had put the time into research, he would have learned that the idea was a bust. The last time we spoke, I learned that his investment had failed to pay off. Worse, he had gotten a loan to keep the business afloat and his growing debt was eating him alive every month.

If you're considering going into business with a partner, here's more advice: have everything clearly defined in writing upfront, including division of responsibilities, labor, startup costs, exit strategy, etc. For partnerships to be successful, there must be an equal balance of resources, commitment, and energy. When one partner feels as though they're putting more into the business than the other partner, there is trouble ahead.

I am not saying that a partnership cannot work, but I certainly hope you enter into one fully informed. I've witnessed too many friendships ruined over business partnerships.

Lastly, make sure you research thoroughly before you jump into the world of entrepreneurship. The federal government has programs specifically for you. Here are a few websites to check out:

Operation Boots to Business
http://boots2business.org

Small Business Administration Resources for Veterans
http://www.sba.gov/content/veteran-service-disabled-veteran-owned

Small Business Administration Veterans Business Outreach Centers
http://www.sba.gov/content/veterans-business-outreach-centers

CHAPTER 4

Apply Your Military Training to the Job Search

If I could summarize the No. 1 factor for a successful job search in one word, it would be preparation. Preparation is the key that separates those who land good jobs from those who struggle indefinitely to find employment. I tell all of my job-seeking clients that preparation is the single most crucial activity to landing a job.

From the moment you discover your end date, start preparing. Continue preparing by combing through job listings and thinking of what to say during your job interviews. Consider it an ongoing learning process.

I've already mentioned in the previous chapter that you must prepare yourself in every way—mentally, emotionally, physically, financially—for life outside the military. And I've touched on a few concrete ways to prepare for the job search, such as reaching out to people and organizations that want to help. I could give you the same old spiel I give to all my clients. I could say, "Do your homework," "Do the leg work," "Do your research."

But you're a specialized group of people. You've undergone intense physical, technical, and psychological training. So I know that you fully appreciate the value of preparation. Consider it reconnaissance. Your mission is to find a fulfilling job that makes the most of your talents, skills, and experience, that helps you reach your full potential, and that supports you and your family financially. And a successful mission requires intel, right?

Get Moving on the Double

I can't imagine more effective training about urgency than spending time in a combat zone. In your military experience, lives depended upon your ability to move with a sense of urgency. You may have had to analyze situations before figuring out your next step, but you also learned how to make those calls on double time. You moved quickly and with purpose. You didn't allow emotions to slow you down. That was never an option.

Think about what led you to develop your sense of urgency. Your time in the service taught you to fully understand the gravity of the situation. Lives depended on you, and your mission was larger than you. The job search is your new mission, and it is no different. Just as lives depended on the outcome of your previous missions, lives now depend on your ability to earn a living. Opportunities come and go, and if you're not fast enough to grab them, you'll miss out.

Know the Terrain

I'm sure you've heard the wise advice, "Never fight where you've never been," or "Know the terrain." In your job search, the terrain is the employment marketplace and you've got to know your way around. If you completed the FAAB+ exercise in Chapter 1, then you should have a good idea of your target industry and position.

Research the industry, specific companies you'd like to work for, and types of positions that attract you. Gather information and absorb as much as possible. Become a mini expert on that industry and position.

Consider the following questions to help guide you:

- How has that industry changed over the last five years?
- What are some new developments in your industry or prospective company that could lead to opportunities for you in the future?
- Are there current events in the headlines that everyone is talking about? If you want to be part of an industry, you should know what's going on.

The answers to the above questions will give you great fodder for networking events and establish your expertise in your area. Start thinking about how your skills and experience can contribute specifically to those companies you identified. If you're facing a tough industry or company to break into, look for entry-level positions or even internships that will help you get your foot in the door.

* *

Action Items:

- **Set up Google Alerts**. These alerts will e-mail you every time your search terms appear on the Internet. I prefer to narrow my search terms for the news filter rather than the "everything" category Google offers. See what works for you. Narrow your search terms to avoid bringing in too many unrelated results that clutter your inbox. Search for company names or even better, the names of key players at those companies whom you'll try to connect with. Go to www.google.com/alerts to set up your alerts. If you end up with too many alerts that clutter your inbox, I recommend setting up an account at Netvibes.com to organize all your alerts in one place.
- **Find relevant news sources and read them regularly.** Look for trade journals in your industry and subscribe. If you're not sure where to start, I recommend Tradepub.com. I've discovered trade publications I never knew existed: *Food Arts*, *Tire Business*, *Electrical Contractor*, *PM Engineer*. The publishers offer free subscriptions to professionals who qualify, so filling out their surveys to get a free subscription is worth a try. At the very least, you can sign up for a publication's free e-mail newsletter. Tradepub.com also has white papers that anyone can download for free.

* *

Know Your Enemy

This ancient advice from Chinese warrior Sun Tzu holds true and is easier to do today more than ever. Of course, potential employers are not the enemy, but they are the people on the other side of your mission. These are the people you must win over. In order to know your enemy, you must know exactly who they are and understand where they are coming from. So you must take two steps:

1) make your list of companies and company contacts and

2) get inside their heads.

* *

Action Item: Prospective Employers Worksheet

Now it's time to systematically identify the employers and the key people you need to engage. At this point, you might have ideas for potential employers floating around in your head. Grab a pen and paper and start listing companies you want to work for. The beauty of this list is that you can start as soon as you confirm you'll be leaving the military. As you find more information about the organizations and their immediate job openings, prioritize your top choices. Depending on how aggressive your job search is, you could have twenty-five or fifty companies listed as your top choices.

Beware: if you don't have an organized way of documenting information about each employers, you may become overwhelmed and get your facts mixed up. Download the worksheet on the Directional Motivation site called Prospective Employers Worksheet.

Once you've researched companies you'd like to work for, find people who will make valuable connections for you in your journey. Look for company gatekeepers. These are the staffers or the recruiter with ties to the company who will decide whether or not to give you a chance. You can find names and titles of the gatekeepers through websites like LinkedIn and Glassdoor and online databases like ReferenceUSA and Hoovers.[16]

16 Check your local library for free access both and ReferenceUSA and Hoovers.

Using this worksheet will help you get organized, compare employers, and get a better idea of the type of work that will satisfy you.

* *

Get Inside Their Heads

It's not enough to know the basic facts about a company. In order to prepare yourself for this mission, you must know how the employers, HR managers, and recruiters think.

Consider the following:

- What motivates them to work day in and day out?
- What is the biggest source of frustration for them?
- What are their problems?
- What were they hoping for when they posted the job listing?
- What defines success for these people?
- What do you have in common with them?

Put yourself in the position of the gatekeeper. Hiring managers are swamped clicking through e-mails full of résumés and cover letters all competing for attention. An open position at their company means there is a hole and the company is operating below capacity. The current employees are picking up the work of the missing team member. They're stretched thin. And the faster they find the perfect fit, the better they will be at running business as usual.

So from the employer's point of view, the hiring process is painful. They want to get back to the business of their industry. When employers and recruiters see an inbox of several hundred résumés, they're working toward getting that inbox down to zero. The hiring process from the employer side, then, becomes a process of elimination through talking with applicants and screening résumés and applications.

Tom Wolfe writes in *Out of Uniform: Your Guide to a Successful Military-to-Civilian Career Transition*, "Employers look for reasons to say no before they look for reasons to say yes."[17] As you prepare yourself to win over the gatekeepers, keep that in mind. Give them reasons to say "yes" to you.

* *

Action Item: Complete the FAAB+ Sheet

Remember the FAAB+ worksheet you downloaded in Chapter 1? If you've done your recon on your target employers, then you have the information you need to fill in the fourth—and most important—column. In this "+" column, you specifically state what you plan to do to benefit the company you're applying to. Feel free to use some of the wording in the previous columns, as long as you phrase it as though you were talking directly to the employer.

Here are a few examples of the complete FAAB+ exercise to illustrate how one column leads to the next:

Features	Accomplishments	Attributes	Benefits	+ (Plus)
Vehicle driver on deployment in Iraq for seven years	Never hit a landmine or IED. Every transport mission went smoothly.	Alert at all times, places high priority in accuracy	Every person and item that I transported went from Point A to Point B safely.	"I understand this position would require a significant amount of concentration for long periods of time. In my previous job, I was very focused on safety. My job demanded me to stay alert at all times. Now I'm adamant about details and accuracy."

17 Tom Wolfe, *Out of Uniform: Your Guide to a Successful Military-to-Civilian Career Transition* (Washington, DC: Potomac Books, 2011), 32.

Features	Accomplishments	Attributes	Benefits	+ (Plus)
Planned retirement, deployment, and change-of-command ceremonies. Negotiated with suppliers on everything including food, music, speakers, screens, etc. Supervised junior officers who worked as support staff.	Provided meaningful events celebrating the service of fellow military personnel. Planned quality events and created appropriate ambiance using limited budgets. Trained junior officers to do my job. All events ran smoothly.	Organized, meticulous, resourceful at improvising, clear communicator, has the forethought to anticipate problems	I often worked behind the scenes while my supervisor remained at the forefront during events, making speeches, toasts, and welcoming guests. My boss often said I made him look good and he really appreciated that.	"I'm glad to hear that support staffers play a major role in creating your product. In my previous position, I functioned as both a supervisor and support staffer, depending on the project. It gave me a new perspective on planning, teamwork, and quality assurance, which all seem like high priorities here."

* *

Look at Your Situation from the 200,000-Foot Level

Part of knowing the terrain includes familiarizing yourself with bordering areas where you might end up. Remember, this is all part of the preparation phase. You're merely checking things out, so be open-minded. The more you explore, the better equipped you'll be at handling detours along the way.

For example, if you find in your research that there is an overabundance of employees in your desired position at your dream company, do some research on the lower level jobs. Sometimes, all it takes is several months of proving yourself in an entry-level position before your managers realize they need to promote you in order to get the most out of your talents.

Brian Cudmore, a former Marine now working at a civilian job in Oregon, recalled there were times when he was in charge of sixty men while on active duty. Nine months after his EAS[18] date, he started an entry-level position in security for Lawrence Livermore National

18 End of Active Service (U.S. Marine Corps)

Laboratory. He went from managing sixty Marines to a position where 200 other members of his department held higher positions.

But Brian said he never considered it a failure to go from a position of authority to starting over from the bottom. He knew that once he proved himself, he'd get promoted quickly. And he did.

Brian said he thought of it like this: "I've already proven time and time again that I can work my way up. My performance speaks for itself."

I also spoke with a retired E-7 from the Navy who struggled adjusting to work after the military. I'll admit it—it was difficult," said Ross Jewell, now living in Tennessee. His first civilian job out of the military was a retail clerk at Lowe's, which paid $8.75 per hour. He had been hoping to earn at least $10 per hour. Still, he decided to take the job because he needed to support his family, and he believed it would be easier to find a higher paying job while employed. I figured I might as well start earning money now and keep looking," Jewell recalled. "That way, I'll have my head on straight while I look for opportunities."

So Ross took the job at Lowe's and continued networking with family and friends. After only thirty days, he made a connection through his brother-in-law, who had a friend at Unilever, one of the largest consumer goods companies in the world. (Just to give you an idea of the size of this company, Unilever's 400 brands include Ben & Jerry's, Ragu, Lipton, Dove, Q-tips, and I Can't Believe It's Not Butter!.)

The HR manager there had initially considered Ross to be overqualified for the open entry-level job as a tomato washer, but based on his brother-in-law's recommendation, offered Ross a job anyway. The job paid pretty close to what he was earning at Lowe's. It wasn't his dream job, but Ross had done his homework on the company and discovered it was growing and offered employees great benefits. He knew he could work his way up from spraying tomatoes.

Ross volunteered to take the early morning shift because none of his coworkers wanted that shift. He wanted to show what he was willing to do for the company.

Soon after, he was chosen to move to a day shift position and gained valuable experience working with the clean-in-place (CIP) sanitation system. Due to his leadership experience in the military, he moved up from being a sanitation employee to a supervisory role. After several promotions over the next eight years, he is now the maintenance scheduler. These days, he's responsible for managing a 260,000 square foot manufacturing facility.

"When I left the military, most people figured I'd just take an hourly job to make ends meet," Ross said. "But I still wanted to make an impact."

That's what motivated him to continue networking after he got his job at Lowe's. It was more important for him to start at the bottom and let his skills, drive, and passion prove to his employer that he was capable of doing more. It worked exactly the way he had hoped.

Ross firmly believes that people with a military background have a distinct advantage from many in the civilian workforce who merely do enough to get by without the drive and passion. "Military folks have discipline, commitment, and passion that will outshine most others in the workplace," he said. "You just have to consistently perform. You will get noticed—just be patient."

I assure you, success stories like Ross's happen all the time. During my research for this book, I talked with Scott Haas, the talent acquisition manager at ThyssenKrupp Aerospace NA / TMX Aerospace, a global supply chain company for aircraft manufacturers based in

Washington. He told me that it's not uncommon for an employee to start out as a forklift driver, get promoted to a production position, and then advance to supervisory roles. I've personally seen speedy promotions happen in the food and beverage manufacturing industry as well. An employee might come onboard as a production supervisor, and, after proving their leadership skills, move into operations, logistics management, or sales management.

Your research will help manage your expectations and open you up to more possibilities you may not have considered in the past. As you search, always have a big picture perspective. I've said this already: lower level jobs can be your launching pad to your dream job. Get your foot in the door and show your stuff, but don't stop searching for opportunities or networking until you get the long-term position you really want.

Have a Strategy with a Built-in Contingency Plan

Would you ever trust a commanding officer who led his unit entirely based on how the enemy responded? How would your unit feel about a mission if your commanding officer didn't set out a plan from the beginning?

I'm guessing you'd feel pretty uneasy about it, right? Every good soldier knows that strategy is key. Following a strategy keeps you focused on the overall goal even as unexpected complications arise and threaten the mission.

The same is true for your job search. Those who fail are typically those without a strategy. All they do is look through listings and submit résumés. When nobody responds to their applications, they get frustrated. And after a long period of feeling desperate and worthless, they either withdraw from the competition or take the first job offer that comes along. That's the painful process so many job seekers suffer through. That type of search doesn't benefit anyone. It robs you of finding a job you enjoy. It robs you of developing your strengths and reaching your potential. It robs your family of being around someone who takes pride in their work. And it robs the many employers out there who are looking for someone just like you. A solid strategy will keep you in the game until you reach your goal.

If there is one piece of advice that I want you to get out of this book, it is this: be proactive, not reactive. The job seekers that merely apply and wait for responses are reactive. You absolutely must operate from a proactive mindset and take charge of the job search. If your only tactic is to apply and hope someone responds, you are resigning yourself to chance.

Let me explain more about the reactive and proactive mindset, which extends to multiple areas of your life. I have discussed this in my other Directional Motivation books as well. However, since I wrote this book specifically for you military veterans, I'd like to give examples that hopefully resonate with you.

Nolan Ruby, a former Marine now living in South Dakota, laughed when I asked him to explain the proactive mindset. He immediately recalled his Marine Corps days during air alert, when he and his fellow soldiers had regular surprise drills to test their rapid deployment readiness. When their commanding officer called out "J.O.B.," everyone knew it stood for "junk on the bunk." All their rapid deployment gear was supposed to be on the bed, packed and ready for inspection. For some, the J.O.B. call triggered a mad dash of packing.

"It was hilarious watching the same guys going into an all-out scramble to find their uniforms and socks," Nolan said. Every time, Nolan explained, those guys would have sweat dripping from their eyes, terrified at the thought of failing inspection.

But even those that managed to pack quickly risked failing inspection. They were packing the gear they'd been using regularly, which often didn't meet the military's quality requirements.

But why did this have to happen every single time? J.O.B. inspections were no secret. Everybody knew the commanding officer would call out "J.O.B." sooner or later. Nolan—smart guy that he is—had a duplicate duffle bag with brand new gear packed and ready. The "mad scramblers" had opted for the cheaper route and avoided buying the duplicate pack. So every time J.O.B. hit, Nolan "just picked [his] up, placed it on the bed, and smiled at the chaos."

Sure, he spent more money upfront. But consider the tradeoffs: he was ready at all times, never had to worry about passing inspection, and most likely, was seen by his commanding officer as a more competent Marine than the others. Being proactive may cost you in time and money, but the payoff in the end will always be worth the upfront cost.

Here are some other examples that illustrate how the reactive soldier will always fall behind the proactive soldier.

Reactive Soldier	**Proactive Soldier**
In the old days, waited to be drafted and assigned	Enlisted to have a choice of service
Pulls rifle trigger and later discovers it's too dirty to fire	Cleans and inspects rifle regularly
Never volunteers and has a poor attitude. As a result, is given assignments no one wants.	Always volunteers and has a great attitude. As a result, typically gets cherry-picked assignments.
Disorganized and regularly fails inspections. As a result, gets assigned disciplinary tasks.	Organized and typically passes inspections. Is given weekend passes frequently.

Reactive Job Seeker	Proactive Job Seeker
Waits until leaving military to begin search	During downtime in the military, drafts a list of ideal employers, prepares résumé, gathers information on career counseling services from the military and nonprofit organizations
Sends out a few résumés and stops while waiting for responses	Sends numerous résumés regularly and systematically follows up
Fails to seek references until the last minute. Uses friends' names and fails to give those people a heads up. Company then calls the references who are caught off-guard and unable to offer any beneficial information.	Puts some thought into finding the best people to serve as references. Chooses the most credible and relevant people and calls them requesting their permission to be listed. Tells them about the target job and asks them to be prepared with examples of candidate's stellar professionalism. Double-checks their contact information.

Plan around Your End Date

Consider yourself luckier than the majority of civilians who get laid off or fired unexpectedly. Many people are escorted to their workstations to pack their personal items in a cardboard box before leaving for good. If they're lucky, they might get some sort of severance pay. If not, they get paid through the end of that day and are booted out with no time to find their next job.

Most likely, you won't have to worry about leaving the military like that. In fact, many of the ex-service members I spoke with had known they were leaving the military for at least a year before they actually left. That's a huge advantage. I know it's unnerving and you still might feel panicked, but with advanced planning, you'll have everything under control.

Ideally, you should have a job waiting for you before you leave the military. I realize this is easier said than done. Many of you may be resistant to working immediately after your exit date because you have the cushion of a military pension. For those of you who were planning to spend several months off reconnecting with family and friends or taking a much-needed vacation, I know it hurts to hear this, but from an employer's point of view, job candidates become less desirable when they're not working.

Retired Col. David Smith he told me one of his biggest regrets in his job hunt was taking six months off before he started looking for a job. He recalled one particular telephone interview where the interviewer asked him what he was doing at the moment. When David explained he was taking time off, it seemed to turn the interviewer off.

As I said in my book *How to Interview: What Employers Want to Hear in Today's Competitive Job Market*, "Free time is a luxury most people don't have, and if your interviewer gets the sense that you spent your time off napping on the couch, milking your unemployment benefits, you'll suddenly become very unappealing."

TheWiseJobSearch.com has a great explanation of why it's easier to get a job while still employed:

> *Employed candidates who don't need a new job, generally spend their time evaluating the employer as much as the employer is evaluating them. They are more "hard to get." Similar to dating . . . generally the one that's a little harder to get is often perceived as more attractive than the one that's too "easy." To an employer, the hard-to-get candidate is perceived as more confident and professional.*[19]

19 "Why is it easier to get a job when you're employed?" The Wise Job Search, accessed April 7, 2013, http://www.thewisejobsearch.com/2011/11/why-is-it-easier-to-get-job-while-you.html.

As soon as you determine your end date, draft a solid month-to-month action plan for the remainder of your time in the service. Here is my recommendation for a twelve-month action plan. Create one for yourself that accommodates the amount of time you have left.

Twelve Months Out

It's never too early to get yourself in battle-ready mode. If you know you'll be leaving the military in a year, start preparing yourself mentally for transitioning to civilian life. This is where you start thinking about the touchy-feely stuff I mention in Chapter 1 (i.e., recognizing your strengths and weaknesses, adjusting your mindset, getting healthy physically and emotionally, talking with your loved ones about the upcoming transition, etc.).

Think deeply about what you want out of work and life:

- Where do you want to live?
- How much money will you need in order to live there?
- What kinds of jobs and industries are you interested in?

- Are you willing to travel?
- Are you willing to start as an unpaid intern in your industry while working nights and weekends to earn a living?
- Are you willing to start as a temp until you can get a full-time position?

As you can tell by my advice so far, the preparation phase requires much time and attention. So go ahead and start your recon as far ahead as you can. Put your list of potential employers and gatekeepers together.

Remember my earlier point about urgency? This is urgent! The earlier you start your recon, the earlier you'll know what qualifications, skills, certifications, or licenses you might be lacking. If you are a logistics professional, you know that any process has the potential to consume an inordinate amount of time.

Creating your list of companies requires much more than a simple Google search and copying and pasting onto your list. You're spending time qualifying prospective companies, checking out their websites, looking up office locations, and digging up salary information for positions you're interested in. (Payscale.com is a great website for salary data.)

It takes time to find out what types of certifications are required for certain positions. You may have to call people or read through long job descriptions. You'll have to research your options and make many decisions: Should I take the free course offered by the military or should I take a more intensive course I must pay for out-of-pocket? Is there a military program that can assist me financially for this program? When does the next session start? Are there night courses available? Should I take the online course or the classroom training? If I start the coursework on this date, will that give me time to prepare for the exam? How long does it take to get my test results back? How soon will I be able to put the completed certification on my résumé?

If you consider these issues early, you'll have plenty of time to get your questions answered and formulate a plan. Instead of making hurried choices out of panic or desperation, you'll make smart, informed decisions.

Ten Months Out

By this time, you have a better idea of your ideal employer. Draft your résumé targeted to your ideal employer. Are you looking for jobs in multiple industries? Tailor your résumé for each industry—even if it means you'll have spend more time creating several different versions. I discuss résumés more closely in Chapter 5.

Eight Months Out

Get your references in order. Reconnect with former managers, mentors, instructors, and commanding officers. See if they'd be willing to vouch for you. If it's been a long time since you worked with them, be ready to remind them about the dates you worked and what you did. Also, prepare yourself for those conversations by listing a few bullet points you would like them to mention in the event an interested employer inquires about you.

Six Months Out

Start networking and building relationships with people that can help you. I talked about this in Chapter 2. Online networking is an easy place to start. Join professional groups on LinkedIn or local networking groups on Meetup. As I mentioned in Chapter 2, the point of networking is to build relationships, not to ask for jobs outright. So be careful not to be pushy. You'll appear desperate and socially awkward if you meet someone and ask if they are hiring right away.

When you make new connections through online networking, don't stay hidden behind your computer. Send messages to your contacts asking if it would make sense for the two of you to connect. From there, gauge whether it will be beneficial to you to set up phone calls or in-person meetings. Don't be afraid to invite people to chat over coffee.

Four Months Out

Start reaching out to recruiters, career counselors, and mentors for help. Do mock interviews so you can practice talking about yourself, showing people the real you, and testing messages and stories that resonate with future interviewers.

This is also a good time to start posting your résumé on sites like CareerBuilder, Monster, SimplyHired, and Indeed. Those are the most well-known job boards for a wide range of industries. Some industries have job boards that attract applicants from more specialized fields. These industry-specific job boards are easy to find with the help of the Internet. For example, when I did a Google search for "engineer jobs websites," not only did I see several job boards, I also discovered a blog post listing seven of the "best and most effective job search websites for engineers." In this age of unlimited information, somebody out there has most likely published helpful tips for your search.

Three Months Out

Start the heavy lifting. That means hitting it hard with job applications, scheduling interviews and checking in regularly with anyone who is helping you, including your career counselor, recruiter, mentor, or chaplain.

Be Prepared for a Long-Term Engagement

Too often, people give up easily. Consider the job search a full-time job in and of itself. It requires your utmost commitment, professionalism, and belief in yourself. Remember when you thought you wouldn't survive basic training? What was it that made you stick with it? I'm sure it wasn't easy, and I'm sure you wouldn't have come this far if you weren't prepared for a long engagement.

There will be times when you feel like giving up. Even for the most committed job seekers, there may be days when you feel so burned out and disappointed that you can't drag yourself out of bed. Just remember that you're in this for the long haul. If you've ever been assigned to a peacekeeping mission, you understand what I mean by that. You know that the time you invest in building relationships and gaining people's trust is vital to the mission.

I get a kick out of John Kriesel's description of his peacekeeping mission in Kosovo in 2004 from his memoir *Still Standing: The Story of SSG John Kriesel*:

> *Our job is "peacekeeper," which apparently means you walk around town smiling at the locals and sit in the coffee shops massaging a cup of java for an hour or two while looking for anything out of the ordinary and keeping the Serbs and Albanians from killing each other—literally.*[20]

If you have the mindset that the job search is a long-term engagement, you'll understand that setbacks are a natural part of the process. Persistence will pay off in the end. There will be times that test you. When you're repeatedly rejected, your emotions may get the best of you. Hopelessness, fear, frustration, and exhaustion can be paralyzing.

20 Jim Kosmo and John Kriesel, *Still Standing: The Story of SSG John Kriesel* (Minnesota: Beaver's Pond Press, 2010) Kindle Locations 579-581.

Take the emotion out of your job search. Systematize the process by having a solid action plan with daily tasks. The busier you stay, the less you'll be affected by your emotions. This is where your psychological military training comes in.

Schedule time every single day to move forward. Set realistic goals for yourself and plan specific tasks. Here is an example of some doable goals:

- Apply to five jobs per day.
- Aim for two job interviews per week.
- Attend one live networking event or job fair per week. Make connections at those events and schedule at least two meetings or calls per week with your new contacts. Get to know them.
- Check in with your support people (i.e., a mentor, career counselor, recruiter, or chaplain) once a week.
- Set aside an hour a day looking through open job listings.
- Set aside thirty minutes a day networking online.
- Connect with five new people on LinkedIn per day.
- Spend ten minutes three times a week reading your FAAB+ sheet you completed in Chapter 4. In fact, read it any time you feel discouraged.
- Spend ten minutes a day planning out your activities for the following day.
- Spend twenty minutes a week evaluating your activity in the previous week and noting any changes you need to make to

be more productive. (I discuss the importance of doing your own AAR[21] in Chapter 7.)

- Read one news article or report every day related to your industry or professional trade to stay up-to-date.

****

Action Item: Set Your Goals and Plan Your Tasks

Make your list of daily, weekly, and monthly goals and tasks. Add reminders in your calendar.

Some of these goals may be out of your control, such as the number of job interviews you get per week. It's important to set those goals, but it's also important to stay positive even when you don't meet them. When job seekers get hung up on the fact that they didn't score those two interviews in a given week, for example, they tend to get depressed and stop their job hunting activities altogether. That's the worst thing you can do.

As a recruiter, I set my goal to place three job seekers in a position every month. That way, I can schedule around those goals and make projections for the business. I don't hit that number of placements every single month. I may go below that number some months, yet exceed that goal in other months.

The goal you set for yourself is not a guarantee. I stay consistent with supporting activities such as networking and researching new outlets, which contribute to my placements in the following months. In other words, even when things don't turn out as planned, I know that good things happen when I stay busy and focused on pursuing my goals. In sales, we call this "filling your pipeline." The same will happen for you in your job search. As long as you continue to fill up your pipeline, something will come through.

21 after-action review

Lastly, I'd like to reiterate another part of your strategy. This proactive job search strategy requires you to process a ton of information. Without an organized system, you'll easily start mixing up companies, gatekeepers, due dates, products, and services. You must keep all of this information in order, so create a system that works for you.

I highly recommend that you check out the free worksheets available for download at www.directionalmotivation.com. Earlier in this book, I refer to the Prospective Employers Worksheet to help you get organized as you narrow down your ideal employers. When you begin interviewing with companies about three months away from your military departure date, you'll be learning even more about each company. This is the critical stage. If you're landing multiple interviews with companies in the same industry, you'll definitely want a system of recording information before *and* after your interviews. The best worksheets for this stage are the Interview Tracker Worksheet and the Employer Assessment Worksheet. Use the Interview Tracker Worksheet to help you prepare for the interview and as a reference in case you get invited for a second interview. After you've done the interview, fill out the Employer Assessment Worksheet to collect your initial thoughts on how well the position and the company suit you.

Now that you've successfully applied your military mindset to the job search, remember that the strategy goes far beyond the moment you land that job. When designing your plan, remember that part of the plan may include working your way up from entry-level positions to your dream job.

CHAPTER 5

Crafting Killer Résumés for Civilian Employment

Many employers have posed this rhetorical question to me: "Why would I hire a military person? They are like government workers, justifying their existence with numbers and acronyms I don't understand. I need an action person. The last thing I need is some paper pusher."

When civilian employers receive eight-page résumés filled with military jargon and figures, it only reinforces their skepticism about hiring military personnel. In fact, I distinctly recall one employer complaining to me about having wasted his time with a résumé. He said, "I read the whole stinkin' thing. Why? I have no idea. I didn't know anything more about this individual than when I started." That statement has stuck with me for years.

In the previous chapter, I told you to think from the employer's perspective. Hiring is a nuisance that must be done to support the company's larger goal to thrive in its industry. For many employers, the hiring process is their worst nightmare. They would much rather be doing work related to their industry, whether it's manufacturing, distribution, or logistics.

When employers are scrolling through résumés, they are looking for people they would like to meet. They want employees who share the same values as their company. Your résumé is a snapshot of your professional life. It can't possibly contain every detail and experience that demonstrates your abilities. If written correctly, however, your résumé will trigger curiosity about you. It won't be the deciding factor that gets you the job, but it will nudge the hiring manager to think, *Hmm, I want to meet this person. Let's schedule an interview.*

So nudge the employer in that direction. Make that person's life easier. Help the harried, stressed employer quickly identify you and the value you would bring to their organization.

Please note: the advice I offer in this chapter is specifically for those seeking civilian employment. Those seeking work as defense or government contractors do not need to "demilitarize" their résumés.

Optimize Your Résumé and Beat the "Black Hole"

Technology has drastically changed the job application process. In order to get a pair of eyes to actually read your résumé, the résumé must make it past the filters of applicant-tracking systems. In other words, robots are the first line of defense for employers being inundated with résumés.

It's been estimated that over 90 percent of Fortune 500 companies use applicant-tracking systems to assist them in sorting through résumés, according to an IBM expert quoted in the *Wall Street Journal*. But big corporations aren't the only ones using these automated systems to filter out résumés. Recruiters and small companies also use them. "Only 19 percent of hiring managers at small companies look at a majority of the résumés they receive, and 47 percent say they review just a few," according to the *Wall Street Journal*, which referenced Information Strategies Inc.[22]

22 Lauren Weber, "Your Résumé vs. Oblivion: Inundated Companies Resort to Software to Sift Job Applications for Right Skills," *Wall Street Journal*, January 24, 2012, http://online.wsj.com/article/SB10001424052970204624204577178941034941330.html.

If you took my advice from the previous chapters and put the time into studying your target companies and industries, you're familiar with the words they use frequently. Study the job listings and websites of the employers on your list. Get a good grasp of the language they use. Observe the phrases, keywords, and tone.

For example, when I read through job listings for the position of project coordinator in multiple industries, I see the same keywords: provide support, multi-task, prioritize, communicates with multiple departments, coordinates, schedules meetings, tracks deliverables, monitors deadlines.

Use job listings as your cheat sheet! Not only do listings reveal the companies' priorities for each role, they also give you the keywords and key phrases that will help keep your résumé from getting lost in the automated systems.

OptimalResume.com advises job seekers to look for the following target keywords:

1) a technical skill, job terminology, or specialization
2) title, type of position, role or department
3) a certification, tool used, specific experience[23]

Oftentimes, people in the military have been using military language to describe what they do because they have heard those keywords so often that they've become ingrained in their vocabulary. If you stick to military terms in your résumé and you're applying for civilian jobs, I guarantee your résumé will get lost in the "black hole" of the automated filtering system. Your résumé might as well be written in a foreign language because the system will not recognize those terms.

---

23 "Optimizing Your Resume for Scanning and Tracking Systems," OptimalResume.com, accessed April 14, 2013, http://www.montclair.edu/media/montclairedu/careerservices/pdfs/OptimalsScannedresumes-1.pdf.

But, by using the language from job listings, you incorporate the terminology from your target employers. And as an added benefit, you'll inherently be better prepared to speak intelligently about your target industry if you land a job interview.

Writing your résumé doesn't have to be a laborious, headache-inducing process. Once you see how your skills and job responsibilities in the military can translate into the civilian jobs that you're aiming for, the résumé writing will get easier.

How Military Résumés Go Wrong

I review more than 200 résumés every day and I notice that résumés from military folks have common pitfalls. What happens when these types of résumés find their way to a civilian employer's desk? In most cases, they end up in the trash bin or buried in the inbox. Your skills and talents are too valuable to end up in no man's land, so give employers a reason to hold onto your résumé.

Here are some of the common mistakes I see in military résumés:

Acronyms and Military Jargon → Ditch Them

After spending any amount of time in the military, I'm sure it's natural for military acronyms to become part of your everyday vernacular. But when you use acronyms in your résumé and any other communications with civilian employers (e.g., e-mails, phone calls, job interviews), you're speaking a foreign language. Employers don't want to have to ask or research what an acronym represents. It's your responsibility to make sure you're conveying information clearly.

To be frank, it's more annoying than anything else to see an acronym in a résumé. It shows the applicant's laziness and inability to anticipate that the acronym might be a stumbling block for the employer.

Here's a line taken from the top section of a military résumé: "I am a Certified DOD Mediator to hear EO complaints."

Leave the certification for the bottom of the résumé. In the body, the employer is more interested in hearing about the quality of work you've done. Here is what he's probably thinking, *Tell me the details of your work as a mediator. Give me a glimpse of the types of disputes you mediated and how you resolved them. And by the way, I know DOD means Department of Defense, but what the heck is an 'EO complaint'?*

Military Vocabulary → Translate for the Average Person

Aspects of the corporate world are actually quite similar to the military. But when you use a different set of vocabulary, you end up making your background seem alien. For example, when you use verbs like "command" and "order" in your résumé to describe your job function, the person reviewing it might envision a dictatorial drill sergeant. You'll give the impression that the people you managed obeyed you only because you were their superior—not someone they truly respected as a leader. Instead, use verbs that demonstrate your ability to work and communicate with people and their diverse perspectives.

Take a look at the chart on the following page for ways to translate your "military speak" for civilian employers.

Military Terms	Civilian Terms
colonel, lieutenant colonel, major general, lieutenant general, general, division commander	senior manager, member of executive management
command, order	lead, champion, train, direct, implement, support
duty	responsibility
mission	goal, objective
patrol	monitor
platoon leader, platoon sergeant, company commander, directorate	department head, department manager
programs (when used as a stream of money, e.g., program for maintenance, buying new vehicles, helicopters)	resources, budget
section chief	team leader
superior, commanding officer, commander	supervisor, manager
unit	team

From the very beginning of the process, translate as much of your experience as possible into civilian language. This applies to all your communication with potential employers, including your résumé, e-mails, conversations, and of course, job interviews.

Too Many Numbers, Too Little Explanation

Numbers aren't necessarily bad. If they demonstrate something meaningful about your previous experiences (e.g. you introduced a new policy that reduced processing time by 30 percent), then include them. But often in the military, some numbers are so intimidating that they deplete the importance of the accomplishment you're trying to showcase. For example, if a veteran says he was responsible for 200 soldiers, the employer would know he couldn't have possibly had much personal contact with all 200 of them. But if he mentioned that he trained five sergeants to lead their groups of forty soldiers each, the statement is more meaningful.

Overemphasis on Technical Skills → Show Your Soft Skills

If you're applying for a technical position, your résumé should play up your technical skills. But you're not a robot. You have a personality and internal drive that fuels your technical aptitude. Make sure that comes across in your résumé. No matter what job you're applying for, employers want to see soft skills, too, such as leadership style, communication skills, motivation to make a difference, and more.

Lengthiness, Longwinded Language → Be Concise, Get to the Point

No matter how many years of experience you've had, no one should have a résumé that's more than two pages. If you're applying for a technical job and want to highlight specific projects, I recommend attaching a separate sheet of case studies or projects.

Too many résumés are often packed with words, but say very little. When I work with job seekers from the military and the government, they tend to replicate information from their military file. They also approach the résumé as a venue for justifying how they've spent their time so far. I've come across résumés the length of research papers, explaining job duties in mind-numbing detail. In certain situations, for example, if you're applying for defense or government contractor positions, those facts and figures are warranted. But if you're aiming to get a job in the civilian world, a résumé with too much information won't get you anywhere.

You never want the person reviewing your résumé to feel frustrated, overwhelmed, or lost. If the reviewer gets bored reading your résumé, it might give off the impression you're dull or bland. If the reviewer gets confused reading your résumé, it might give the impression that you're not a clear communicator or simply not bright.

The best way to avoid this is to be concise. Get straight to the point. Use action words to bring life to the résumé using as few words as possible. Every word on your résumé occupies valuable space. Don't waste space on meaningless words. You don't even need full sentences! Use bulleted lists where appropriate.

Bureaucratic Statements→ Simple Is Better

Oftentimes, job seekers will literally copy and paste elements of their military job descriptions onto their résumés. **Big mistake.** The people who wrote those descriptions aren't necessarily the best communicators. When you're applying for civilian jobs, your résumé should enable the average person to visualize and understand exactly what you do.

Here are two examples of bureaucratic language that must be broken down:

Line from résumé: "Executed ground/air patrol in order to enforce 24 hour surveillance of RCA/MKLP[24] activities."

Why it doesn't work: This statement goes around in a circle. It says you did one thing in order to do the same thing.

Try this: "Monitored enemy army activities through ground and air patrol. Provided border control support."

Line from résumé: "Facilitated coordination of logistical process."

Why it doesn't work: I have no idea what this statement is trying to say. "Facilitate" and "coordinate" in the same statement are redundant. "Logistical process" could have a dozen different meanings. As the reader, I cannot grasp what exactly this person did. I need to understand what logistics were involved.

---

24 I've changed the acronyms here and in other resume examples to protect the privacy of the resume holders.

Try this: "Ensured on-time delivery of food and toiletry items to twenty-five combat zones throughout the Middle East."

"So What?" Statements → Tell Me Why It Matters

Sometimes, I read a statement in a résumé and think to myself, "So what?" Then I prod the candidate for more information and realize that they simply didn't highlight the significant part of that experience. Former Marine Nolan Ruby gave this great advice: Employers just don't know how to interpret military accomplishments into their own private companies. It's up to you to explain it.

Here are a few more examples taken from real résumés, which I've also altered for the sake of privacy:

Line from résumé: "Appointed as a Member of the MLB Ambassadors Group by Navy Chief of Staff"

Recruiter's initial thought: *So you were granted access to this group. So what? What does it say about you? I've never heard of this group.*

What I discovered: After questioning my client about this group (whose name I changed), I realized that only those who performed at the top levels were appointed. So I had this person add more detail about what she did to reach that level of achievement.

Line from résumé: "Participated in Annual SDBE Sea Ops Plan Conference"

Recruiter's initial thought: *So you went to a conference. So what? Typically, conferences are open to anyone willing to pay the registration fee.*

What I discovered: After questioning my client about what happened at the conference, I learned that he collaborated with service members to draft a plan to expedite the process of doing aircraft maintenance checks.

Line from résumé: "Annually conducted 300 written, verbal, and physical evaluations of Security Forces military to complete their certification and/or validate that required training is being conducted."

Recruiter's initial thought: *I have no idea what kind of work goes into these evaluations, so it's difficult for me to gauge the importance of the number 300. Does this candidate spend one hour or eight hours on each evaluation? What skills do they use to accurately assess each person? How closely does this person work with the people under evaluation? Do they help guide those 300 people? How? I need to understand the impact they made for the people evaluated.*

What I discovered: Nothing. I never called this applicant. This statement alone included two big turn-offs: a big number and a statement that means nothing to a civilian.

Highlighting Decades of Military Service Makes You Look Old

It's perfectly understandable why you might feel proud of having served, say, twenty years in the military. But don't create additional hurdles through misconceptions by explicitly stating at the top of your résumé that you had a twenty-year career in the armed forces. When employers see that a person has held a position for a couple of decades, they automatically assume the candidate must be old when, in fact, the individual could be as young as thirty-eight if they joined right out of high school. Let the employers see your skills and experience first and do the math later. Don't give them an easy reason to reject you. If you've spent many years in the military, I recommend writing "extensive experience" instead of the number of years served.

The Word "Retired" Evokes Undesirable Assumptions

For many people, retirement conjures up images of sixty-something perpetual vacationers sipping piña coladas in Florida. The assumption is that they've spent multiple decades in their careers and are ready to sit back and enjoy their golden years. They're receiving retirement benefits, so whatever job they're applying for now is a nice way to pad their current income. They don't *need* this job, so they won't try as hard as the other applicants who are still in mid-career.

Obviously, I don't buy into this stereotype. But I'm also a realist. Like I said before, don't give employers an easy reason to reject you. Leave the word "retired" out of your résumé.

* *

So far, I've given you an insider's perspective of why civilian employers are resistant to hiring ex-military personnel. Doesn't it make sense, then, to craft a résumé that shoots down every possible reason employers might feel iffy about you?

Here are some additional tips:

Create Multiple Versions

I've already mentioned that if you are looking for jobs in multiple industries, you'll need to tailor your résumé for each industry. We've already pointed out the different languages of the military world and civilian world. Now think of the various industries in the same way. Law firm staffers talk very differently from tech startups. People in the medical field use different terminology from people in manufacturing. The more you know about your ideal employers, the better you will be at determining what they are looking for, and therefore, what to include in your résumé.

Use a Hybrid Profile-Objective-Company (POC) Heading

I often see résumés with the applicant's objective listed at the top. Here's a typical example: "To secure employment as a project manager at an information technology firm." As an executive recruiter who knows how hiring managers think, this type of statement is not helpful. It tells the employer what you want, not what you can offer.

On the other hand, I've also seen résumés with a profile heading that highlights key skills, qualifications or summarizes the applicant's experience in a sentence. The profile heading can be helpful, but it runs the risk of repeating included in the résumé.

I propose a hybrid model that incorporates the applicant's profile, their objective, and a complimentary description of the company the applicant is applying for. Think of it as similar to the value statement I describe in Chapter 2.

Here's an example of the hybrid POC heading: "Electrical designer with expertise in automation and relay logic systems searching for an innovative manufacturing company."

Lacking Education? Highlight Your Professional Development

If you've never completed high school or college and you're wondering what to list in the education section of the résumé, no need to worry. I recommend following the advice from Monster Résumé Expert Kim Isaacs, which is to create a Professional Development Section where you highlight vocational training, certifications, courses, even seminars or conferences you attended.[25]

If you did not complete high school and instead, passed the G.E.D., don't include the G.E.D. on your résumé. Employers tend to assume

25 Kim Isaacs, "Resume Dilemma: No Degree" Monster.com, accessed May 19, 2013, http://career-advice.monster.com/resumes-cover-letters/resume-writing-tips/resume-dilemma-no-degree/article.aspx.

that candidates graduated from high school. You may hear differing opinions on this from other career counselors, but I firmly believe it's better not to highlight the fact that you did not earn a high school diploma.

Avoid Unnecessary Personal Information

There's no need to include your social security number, height, weight, or picture.

* *

Once you have posted your résumé on various job boards, you'll have edits and additional experiences. Remember to keep all of your résumés updated, which maintains your "active" status. Sometimes, when I'm searching through résumés on sites like CareerBuilder, I see résumés with eight months of no activity. In those cases, I assume the people are no longer searching for a job, so I bypass their résumés.

To recap, your résumé should be concise and effective in capturing the employer's attention. For examples of effective résumés and recommended formats, go to www.directionalmotivation.com.[26]

26 Go to the Military tab and you'll find the Résumés icon.

CHAPTER 6
The Job Interview

If you've been contacted for a job interview, congratulations! You've already impressed the person in charge of screening applicants. There is something about you that made the hiring manager think, *I want to meet this person.* Now you're among a select group of applicants attempting to win over the interviewer.

The interview stage is the point where your preparation work (i.e., research, mock interviews, Directional Motivation exercises) will pay off. It is the single most important part of the job search process. And because of that, I'm structuring this chapter somewhat like a military operation plan.

Military Operation Plan

Mission
Show the interviewer "the real you." In the military, you respect the rank, then decide if you respect the person. In the civilian world, your rank is not as important as the person you are behind the rank.

References

This includes your résumé, your Directional Motivation exercises, your company worksheets, and any other information you've gathered about the company.

Assessment Element

First, let's assess the mistakes that other military veterans have made, so that you don't make the same mistakes.

Here's a story from Chaplain Anderson that shows why job interviewers and veterans just don't click. He was counseling a soldier who'd been unsuccessful at landing a job. So the chaplain offered to do a mock interview. Here's how it went:

Interviewer: What do you do?

Interviewee: I'm an 88 mic.

Interviewer: Well, what's that? Could you explain to me?

Interviewee: What do you mean? I'm an 88 mic.

Interviewer: What does an 88 mic do?

Interviewee: I drive trucks.

Interviewer: What kind of trucks?

Interviewee: Whatever they want me to drive.

The applicant most likely figured, *I drove trucks for the Army. Now I'm applying for a job as a truck driver. What more do they need to know?*

Imagine yourself on the other side of the conversation. You're the interviewer trying to learn more about this person. You're trying to discover what he can offer, what motivates him. You're evaluating him to see if he'll fit in with the team and if he'll have a future with the company beyond this position. What did he do wrong? How did he make your job more difficult?

Let's see . . . He did nothing more than answer questions. He wrongfully assumed the interviewer knew the definition of an 88 mic and got noticeably impatient when the interviewer didn't understand. He repeatedly forced the interviewer to waste time asking for clarification. What would compel the interviewer to learn more about this person? If I were interviewing that 88 mic, I would have ended the interview right then and moved on to the next candidate. None of his answers showed, experience, or character traits that could benefit any company.

As a recruiter, I've often found myself in similar situations when trying to match up veterans with companies that are hiring. The feedback I hear most often from hiring managers who have just interviewed a military veteran is that they're too rigid. Of course, there are many reasons behind this (e.g. a buzz cut, an emotionless face, answers that end at "Yes, sir," "No, ma'am").

All those military acronyms and jargon just don't make any sense for us in the civilian world. When your interviewers don't understand you or relate to you, the interview is essentially over. The opportunity to engage them in meaningful conversation and show them the real you is lost. You won't be able to illustrate the value you could bring to their organizations.

Other times, my military job seekers come prepared to speak about their experience, but they end up spewing out numbers, dollar amounts, and tedious information. Someone fresh out of the military might answer the typical interview starter "Tell me about yourself," like this: "Sir, I was regional commander of Unit 892 with responsibility over 400 men, fifteen battalions, and $500 million of government-issued tanks and weaponry."

In my meetings with military candidates, introductions like those typically take ten to fifteen minutes. It seems as though the candidates don't even stop to take a breath! As the interviewer, I don't have the opportunity to interject myself into the conversation and therefore, can't connect with the applicant.

In my book *How to Interview: What Employers Want to Hear in Today's Competitive Job Market*, I explain that facts and figures don't tell the story of who you really are. Let me explain. If I were to tell you that I have been an executive recruiter for over twenty years, placed 798 candidates, and worked with twenty-seven Fortune 500 companies in ten states, can you really get a sense of my internal drive? No.

What if, instead, I said this during the interview: "I'm passionate about making a difference in people's lives. In my professional life, I make an impact by helping job seekers find work. In my personal life, I've been volunteering as a prison chaplain for the last twenty years."

Do you see the tremendous difference it makes when you bring in the "real you" into the conversation? Now that we've assessed the mistakes of other job candidates, let's move on to examining the purpose behind the interview.

Situation: The Real Purpose of the Job Interview

From my experience counseling both military and civilian job candidates, I've discovered that most civilians dread job interviews because they feel intimidated by the employers. On the other hand, the military veterans who've had bad interview experiences typically dread the process for a different reason: they often end up feeling frustrated over questions they don't know how to answer. They think, *What's the point of inquiring about all those useless details? I just want to tell them what they need to know. Nothing more, nothing less.*

Military people are accustomed to communicating differently. Retired Army officer Tim Mariner explained the communication divide between service members and civilians:

> *Military people are direct and to-the-point. People take offense to that. They say that military people are too "in-your-face." But we're just used to getting the job done. Lives depend on it. In the service, we needed to be able to analyze a situation and make a decision very quickly. In a nonthreatening environment, people have more time.*

I understand where you're coming from. But when you're talking to civilian hiring managers who are giving you a golden opportunity, you need to communicate on *their* terms. When the interviewer asks a question, that person is hoping for the answer to reveal deeper qualities and characteristics about you. This is the real purpose of the interview. Employers want to see your heart and passion—not your military identity or a regurgitation of your résumé. Your résumé already shows your educational background, professional certifications, and technical skills. Your previous rank, awards, and the headcount of those that reported to you are not the real you. The interview is your chance to show your personality and character. So loosen up and smile!

No matter what position you're applying for, employers are looking for personal attributes like integrity, adaptability, resilience, and reliability. They want people who can be part of a team and effectively communicate with their team members. These are the golden intangibles that can only come through in the way you present yourself.

Assumptions

Before we move on to interview strategies, I want to make sure you grasp several basic principles:

1) You, the candidate, are responsible for showing the interviewer the value you bring to the organization quickly and precisely. If you completed the FAAB+ exercise in Chapter 1, you should have a clear vision of what you have to offer.

2) The fact that you served in the military does not make you more qualified or worthy of getting that job than the next candidate. I warn against the entitlement mentality earlier in this book, but it warrants another mention when it comes to interviews. As former Army officer Aaron Curtis joked, "You may have your own action figure coming out. That's great. No one cares." Your military badges and medals are commendable, of course, but ultimately, the employer wants to know, *Can you solve my problem right now?*

3) Engaging the interviewer is equally as important as relaying information about yourself. It's critical to make that connection. During the job interview, this is the position you must take: the interviewer is the most important person on the face of the planet and that company is the most exciting place to work. If you did your research in Chapter 4 on the company and the person interviewing you, this will be easy. Show the interviewer that you went beyond

the job listing and did your own research. Tell the interviewer what attracted you to that company and that position.

4) The interview is not solely an exchange of data. If employers simply wanted information about your skills and qualifications, they would save time and money by e-mailing you the questions and asking you to respond in writing. Or the decision might be based solely on how well you do on a test. Employers invite you for an interview because they want to observe you in person and converse with you.

* *

Interview Prep Action Item #1:
Review the FAAB+ worksheet you completed in chapters 1 and 4. Think of the characteristics that set you apart from the others. What makes you different? What drives you? What are you passionate about?

Here's a statement to fill in the blanks and practice:

"The people who know me best would describe me as more than your average ______ because I am ___________ and because I spend time ___________."

Here are a few examples to show you the power of this simple sentence:

"The people who know me best would describe me as more than your average Navy intelligence officer because I am excruciatingly thorough and because I spend time consulting my sources in-person when possible."

"The people who know me best would describe me as more than your average Air Force technical sergeant because I am a persistent team leader and because I spend time understanding where my team is coming from."

"The people who know me best would describe me as more than your average Navy seaman apprentice because I am curious and because I spend time investigating every detail of my assignments."

* *

Execution Strategies:

Tell stories. They are more powerful than facts.

I'd like you to recall the introduction of this book, where I list statements from employers who have objected to hiring people from the military. This list hopefully served as an eye-opener for you, as well as a cheat sheet on the specific stereotypes to overcome. Telling stories is the best way to connect with the interviewer and change any preconceived notions that person may have about ex-military personnel.

Tom Wolfe explains the role of stories in the job interview:

> *Many companies look at it like this: What you have done is not nearly as important as how well you have done it. Previous success is an excellent indicator of potential success, even if the goals of the new organization differ from those of the former one.*[27]

If you're one of the hundreds of thousands of ex-military personnel who have never held leadership roles, this is an especially helpful insight. John Kriesel mentioned to me that much of his time in the military was spent as an infantryman. He was a regular machine gunner, rifleman, and infantry vehicle driver. "It doesn't matter if

27 Wolfe, *Out of Uniform*, 12.

you weren't in charge of fifty men," Kriesel said. "Talk about why you loved your job, why you were great at it, and how you're going to transfer that mentality, that experience, and that passion to your new job."

Telling stories is also an effective strategy for those who *have* held military leadership positions. One of the stereotypes is that in the military, commanding officers don't make good team players because all they have to do is shout orders and their subordinates will obey.

Naturally, if you're on the battlefield, you don't ask for a group decision, as ex-Army Sgt. Tim Mariner pointed out. But you and I both know effective military leaders do seek input from people in the lower ranks. Tim explained that as a commanding officer, he would often get together with junior leaders and formulate plans together. So how can you get that point across? Prove it. Think of the times you collaborated with groups of people and tell those stories to your interviewer. Use storytelling as a tool to shoot down stereotypes.

Focus on Telling the "How"

The interviewer has already reviewed your résumé and knows the basic facts about your professional life so far. Now they want to know your internal motivators. Help them out by explaining how you did your job. Even when they don't specifically ask "how," include that in your responses: *how* you accomplished goals, *how* you came up with great ideas, *how* you got yourself out of sticky situations, *how* you managed other people, etc.

Leadership is not about the number of people who reported to you. It's about *how* you led, *how* you earned the respect of your peers and those who reported to you, *how* you created a common vision, *how* you connected with people.

Let's take David Smith's background as another example. He had experience in the Army managing inventory of vehicle repair parts. He didn't have experience in retail distribution, but he knew that his skills managing inventory would be transferrable to any industry. He didn't need any coaching from me on explaining how his skills would benefit a civilian employer. He explained it very clearly: "It doesn't matter if the inventory is made up of cans of hairspray or trucks. It's not what you manage. It's how you manage it. You manage based on demand."

In most cases, clearly explaining to your interviewer *how* you did your job is even more important than explaining *what* the job entailed.

Explain the "Why"

I once had an ex-military candidate from California looking for a production supervisor position who told me, "Some people love me; some people hate me. That's just the way I am." He stopped right there. I knew a hiring manager would probably not be interested in hearing more after that statement. But I thought he might have more to offer, so I replied, "Why?"

"Some people see me as a hard ass," the candidate explained with another one-liner.

I considered ending the conversation right then, but for some reason, I prodded a bit more. It turned out this fellow had much to offer. He described his work as a Navy Hospital Corpsman, which required supervising twenty-six people, communicating in diverse environments, and serving thousands of patients. As we talked, I discovered that he was very detail-oriented and conscientious. He shared anecdotes about how his team often made jokes about his seemingly "over the top" expectations. Because of those high expectations, though, his team consistently earned superior rankings and, despite the jokes, it seemed like they appreciated his perfectionism.

The "hate" he had mentioned at the beginning of our conversation was, in reality, admiration and respect from his team. Luckily, I was not a hiring manager and he was not interviewing for a particular position in that situation. However, without explaining the essential "why" of his statements, he could have easily given someone the wrong impression of himself.

Describe the Qualities, Skills, and Experience That Will Serve the Employer

While the mission of the interview is to show the "real you," also keep in mind that the interviewer cares only about the "real you" in the context of what you can do for the company. Always put yourself in the place of the interviewer and think, *If I were running this company, why would I hire this person?*

Sadly, I have known many ex-military personnel applying for jobs who have told interviewers, "I just want some way to finish out my career," or worse, "I've got a few good years left in me." If you were the employer, would you even consider hiring a candidate who said that? Of course not. From the employer's point of view, even if it seemed obvious that you were capable of doing a good job, those statements would give the impression that you had no interest in serving the employer—only in serving yourself.

I have already discussed at length the importance of thoroughly researching your prospects. If an employer contacts you for a job interview, you must get a firm understanding of its mission, goals, priorities, services, products, customers, and more. So while you may be extremely proud of your strengths in a certain area, craft your statements to show how you can benefit the company.

Former Marine Brian Cudmore gave me a perfect example of this. He was interviewing for a position as a hospital staffer in charge of distributing equipment and supplies to multiple departments. He never mentioned that he was an expert in eight weapons systems. He did not talk explicitly about his ability to shoot people from a mile away or how easy it was for him to blow holes in doors and windows. He might have been duly proud of those skills, but he knew they would be irrelevant for a job at a hospital. Instead, he indirectly referenced those skills in a way that captured his interviewer's attention, kept the interviewer engaged, and stayed in line with the hospital's goal

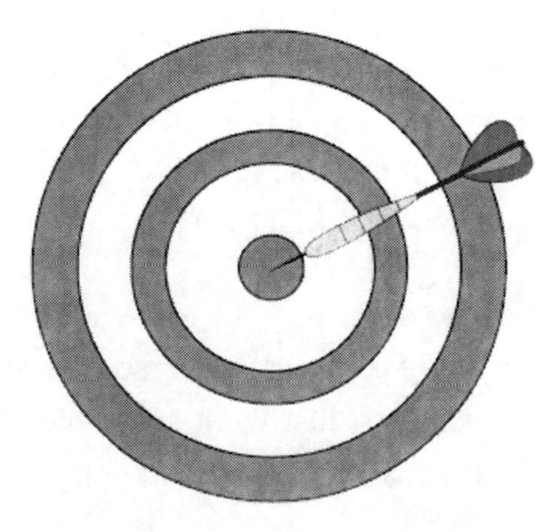

of providing excellent customer service to its patients. This is what he said: "I have extreme patience. I'm diligent and hardworking. I can read multiple impacts to a scenario, factor in on the target, and achieve the goals I set for myself."

He explained to me that he was actually describing himself while pointing a gun at a target 800 yards away. But of course, the interviewer would not have known that. "It's the process that you need to focus on," Cudmore said, "not the end result."

Make Sure the Interviewer Understands Your Message

Think about this for a moment: Do you recall the person you were before you joined the military? What did you envision happening in a soldier's day-to-day life? Most likely, your limited knowledge about the military was based on news stories, movies, or books, right? When I was young, I watched TV shows like *M*A*S*H* and *Hogan's Heroes*. I ate up war movies like *The Dirty Dozen* and *Lawrence of Arabia*. For many years, all I knew about the military came from entertainment. Like that younger me, most civilians have no idea what the average day looks like for a service member.

Give the interviewer the courtesy of being clear. I've said this many times already, but it bears repeating: it's your responsibility to get the interviewer to understand your valuable experience in the military and how that experience can benefit their organization.

One simple key to getting a sense of whether or not you are being clearly understood is to observe your interviewer's facial expressions. Furrowed eyebrows or a one-eyed squint are dead giveaways. Feel free to ask the interviewer politely if you're being clear enough. Or stop and say, "Let me explain this differently" or, "In other words," and then try to simplify without losing the core of your message.

Make civilian analogies to military situations that are more familiar to the interviewer or easier to visualize. Review the military-to-civilian chart in Chapter 5 and demilitarize your language.

Trust me, your interviewer will notice your perceptive ability and impressive communication skills—both highly prized skills in the civilian world. Remember, clarity is key.

Be Aware of Your Own Face

It's easy to forget about your own facial expression, especially during a job interview. But your face is one of your most important tools to combat the preconceived notion many civilian employers have that military veterans are too rigid, robotic, or stoic. Don't reinforce that stereotype—debunk it! Give the interviewers a friendly, smiling face and maintain good eye contact. Not only is smiling contagious, it will also keep you energized and positive throughout the interview.

A Note on Confidence

Confidence is definitely an important attribute. You should exhibit confidence in your abilities. In fact, the interview is a prime opportunity to show how you stand out from your competition. However, be very careful not to project egotism, bravado, or narcissism. Former Marine Brian Cudmore addressed this point perfectly:

> *In the military, you have confidence that you'll be able to handle any situation. While that may be unrealistic, for the most part, you believe that you can. That's what you're trained to do. You do it or you don't make it out. So when someone asks, "Can you do this mission?" you say, "I'll do this mission better than anyone else."*

In the civilian world, that attitude could come off as brash or cocky. Keep in mind that employers want people who are eager to learn and be part of a team. This is one of the many reasons why practicing mock interviews with a mentor, recruiter, career counselor, or military chaplain is so important. Ask your mock interviewer for honest feedback about this particular area and determine if you need to tone down your language or nonverbal signals.

Ask Questions

Employers will usually give the applicant an opportunity to ask questions about the position or the company. This is another chance for you to show your sincere enthusiasm for the position and the energy you would bring to the company. Ask relevant questions about the expectations of the position, the history and culture of the company, and the background of the interviewer.

Here are some examples:

- *What would be an effective way to measure my success here?*
- *I'm interested in learning about the high performers here. What makes them so effective?*
- *I'm curious to understand what drew you to the organization and what keeps you here.*
- *What separates this company from your competition?*
- *What are some of the latest strategic initiatives that will keep your company competitive in the future?*
- *What is a possible career track for a successful employee here?*

- *What would you like to see me accomplish in the first thirty to ninety days working here? How about the first year?*
- *Are there opportunities for to be mentored here? How does it work?*
- *How has this company invested in research and development efforts? What are the company's expectations out of it in the coming years?*

* *

Interview Bloopers

Through the years, I've received all kinds of feedback from hiring managers who have interviewed my candidates. In some of the worst interviews, the hiring managers later quoted the candidates to me and shared their thoughts on why those candidates ruined their chances of getting hired. I typically coach my candidates before their interviews, but sometimes, I'll still get the same feedback. It kills me to see candidates make the same awful statements during job interviews! I often wish I could show people a reel of interview bloopers, so that job seekers can avoid making those mistakes.

Let's take a look at some of the worst comments I've heard candidates make during interviews. I'll explain how employers interpreted those comments and analyze each one. I'll also rework each statement, so you can see how slight changes can make a substantial difference.

Candidate statement:

"I think I have a few good years left."

Employer's Interest Level

This statement is a big turnoff to employers. It sounds like there are just a few vapors left in your tank. Employers are seeking high-energy players.

New and Improved Statement:
"I'm eager to put my skills and experience to work for you."

Employer's Interest Level

Candidate statement:

"I'm sure you can tell from all my experience that this job would be easy for me, but I need a job."

Employer's Interest Level

It sounds like you think the job is below you. Why would the interviewer want to hire someone who will obviously be dissatisfied working there?

New and Improved Statement:
"I may be somewhat overqualified for your position, but in every position that I've held, I've always taken on additional responsibilities that challenge me and allow me to contribute my best to the organization."

Employer's Interest Level

Candidate statement:

"I know I'm not qualified, but I need a job."

Employer's Interest Level

This statement makes you sound desperate. Show your energy and desire to learn. An employer is more likely to consider you for this or other positions if you can show your resourcefulness and determination. Use stories from previous jobs to illustrate these qualities about you.

New and Improved Statement:

"At first glance, it would appear that I'm not qualified, but in two other positions that I've held, my immediate supervisors had initially felt the same way. They both were impressed with how quickly I learned and noted that in my evaluations."

Employer's Interest Level

Candidate statement:

"I'm just looking for a company that I can retire with."

Employer's Interest Level

Although you might be trying to show your loyalty, the interviewer will get the impression that you're looking for nothing more than to ride off into the sunset.

New and Improved Statement:

"My prior supervisors loved my loyalty and commitment to the job and to the people around me. You can count on me to get your job done and set the example for my peers."

Employer's Interest Level

Interview Prep Action Item #2:

Now that you've picked up some interview tips, let's try the next exercise to get you battle ready. Lou Adler, CEO of the recruiting agency The Adler Group, posted this question on LinkedIn as the most important interview question of all time: **What single project or task would you consider the most significant accomplishment in your career so far?**

Think about how you would answer this question and start brainstorming your answer in writing. Next, prepare yourself to answer these likely follow-up questions from the same LinkedIn post:

- Can you give me a detailed overview of the accomplishment?
- Tell me about the company, your title, your position, your role, and the team involved.
- What were the actual results achieved?
- When did it take place and how long did the project take.
- Why you were chosen?
- What were the three to four biggest challenges you faced and how did you deal with them?
- Where did you go the extra mile or take the initiative?
- Walk me through the plan, how you managed to it, and if it was successful.
- Describe the environment and resources.
- Describe your manager's style and whether you liked it or not.
- Describe the technical skills needed to accomplish the objective and how they were used.
- Some of the biggest mistakes you made.

- Aspects of the project you truly enjoyed.
- Aspects you didn't especially care about and how you handled them.
- How you managed and influenced others, with lots of examples.
- How you were managed, coached, and influenced by others, with lots of examples.
- How you changed and grew as a person.
- What you would do differently if you could do it again.
- What type of formal recognition did you receive?[28]

* *

Behavior-Based Interviewing

Now that you know my winning interview techniques, I'd like to introduce you to a specific style of interview questions. Behavior-based interviewing takes real-life situations that you may encounter in the workplace and asks you to provide examples of how you have handled these types of situations in prior settings. Many employers rely heavily on these questions because the answers speak volumes about the job applicant.

However, for many of you transitioning military applicants, these types of questions can be frustrating because they might seem too "touchy-feely." Former Marine Brian Cudmore made me realize just how inconsequential those questions might appear to someone transitioning out of the armed forces. He shared a couple behavior-based questions he had encountered in interviews and what he was thinking.

---

28 Lou Adler, "The Most Important Interview Question of All Time - Part 1," January 17, 2013, Lou Adler's LinkedIn page, accessed April 15, 2013, http://www.linkedin.com/today/post/article/20130117183637-15454-the-most-important-interview-question-of-all-time.

Interviewer: *How do you deal with stressful situations?*

Interviewee's mental images: *me eating dirt, starving, bleeding, or causing someone else to bleed*

Interviewee's unfiltered thoughts: *I've had people shoot at me. When I was twenty-one years old, I was making decisions that could've cost people's lives. Why are you asking me about stress?*

Interviewer: *Can you think of a time that you had to deal with a difficult colleague? How did you handle it?*

Interviewee's unfiltered thoughts: *I punched them in the face, told them to get over themselves and suck it up.*

I get it. In a sense, behavior-based questions reveal the pettiness of the civilian working world. Questions that probe into your thoughts and feelings might seem trivial, but they are actually very relevant. I mention earlier in this chapter that employers are looking for people with integrity, adaptability, resilience, and reliability. Through behavior-based questions, interviewers hope to understand your decision-making ability, critical thinking, and thought processes in order to predict how you will respond to certain life and workplace scenarios.

Following are some common behavior-based interview questions[29]:

1) Tell me about a time when you worked for a difficult supervisor or managed a problematic subordinate. How did you resolve this situation?

What they really want to know: Are you the type of individual that will end up in the fetal position in a difficult environment, or will you

29 I do not provide you specific responses because those must relate to your unique background. However, I do offer insights on what the interviewer is trying to learn about you.

find a way to overcome this situation? Will you blame someone else or take responsibility?

2) Tell me about a situation in which you failed. What did you learn from this experience and how have you applied this lesson in your life?

What they really want to know: Do you persevere, regardless of hurdles? Do you take the pitfalls of life and use them to prepare yourself for challenging situations in the future? Do you view these circumstances as developmental steps, or do you complain that life wasn't fair?

3) Tell me about a time when you proposed an idea to your manager, but your manager did not use it. How did you respond? How did you communicate this development to subordinates and coworkers?

What they really want to know: Will you become bitter when coworkers do not accept or act upon your ideas? Will you convey a negative spirit or attitude to peers and subordinates that will impact morale, or do you keep your spirits high and continue contributing to the team?

4) Tell us about a time in which you were asked to influence a group of people to take a certain course of action. What approach did you use and what was the outcome?

What they really want to know: Are you a leader? Do others trust you, and will people follow you? Can you be put in positions of authority? Are your efforts successful?

5) If you were to start your life over, what changes or adjustments would you make? Why?

What they really want to know: Are you willing to admit possible mistakes? What have you learned from your experiences? How have you applied this knowledge? How perceptive are you to changing trends?

6) Please provide us with a couple of examples in which you made a positive impact in your workplace environment. How would you accomplish this within our organization?

What they really want to know: Do you have personal initiative to make a difference? Are you comfortable with the status quo or do you try to make things better?

7) How do you define leadership? How have you implemented it in your own life? What have been the results?

What they really want to know: Do you believe in building a team environment or are you more of the authoritarian type? Are your answers fluff or can you back them up with clear examples?

8) If you owned your own business and a person like yourself applied, why would you hire that person?

What they really want to know: How do you see yourself? What do you like about yourself?

9) How would you describe your most difficult boss? What changes would you suggest to that boss? What have you learned from the experience of working for this person?

What they really want to know: By describing your most difficult boss, you will demonstrate the issues that they really struggle with. It will also reveal if the source of the problem was the boss or the employee. Will you value the negative experience and change your own management style to avoid making the same mistakes, or will you stick to venting about your old boss?

Unfortunately, I've heard from too many employers that job applicants go to the interview without ever having thought about any of these scenarios. When these behavior-based questions come up, many interviewees have responded with, "I don't think I can answer that," or "Wow, I guess I've never thought about this before."

Use these sample behavior-based questions as a rough guide to help you think of specific examples that would demonstrate your abilities in each of these areas. I also encourage you to visit my website at www.directionalmotivation.com for more interview questions.[30] If you are having trouble in crafting answers, e-mail me at russ@directionalmotivation.com and I will be happy to assist you.

* *

Interview Prep Action Item #3:

Find someone from your support team (e.g., a mentor, career counselor, chaplain, recruiter, family member or friend) and answer the sample questions from this chapter in a mock interview.

* *

Coordinating Logistics

Lastly, never underestimate the importance of planning your schedule and getting the best directions to get to the interview.

1) **Clear your schedule for the entire day** if you are having an on-site interview. If an employer thinks you're a promising candidate, that person may decide to give you a full tour and have you visit with other leaders in the organization. These are good signs! By giving yourself flexibility, you will be in a position to accommodate such requests.

30 Go to the Military tab and click on the Sample Interview Questions icon.

2) **Know the physical location of your interview.** I suggest that you not only map out your route and check traffic patterns a couple of days beforehand, but also do a test drive to your destination. Should you run into an unforeseen problem, always call the employer, briefly explain what happened, and give your anticipated arrival time. Long-winded sob stories are annoying, so keep it short. When you arrive—albeit later than scheduled—be sure to let the interviewer know the effort you put into trying to show up on time. Even if your logistics didn't work out this time, at least you can demonstrate that you did everything in your power to arrive on time.

3) **Be prompt.** Arrive no sooner than fifteen minutes early, but no later than five minutes early. If you arrive more than fifteen minutes before the scheduled time, you may end up sitting for an extended period of time, creating a potentially awkward situation with the receptionist. You also don't want to look desperate.

Chapter 7

Dealing with Rejection by Maintaining Momentum

I realize that this book is giving you more work than you might have anticipated. Sometimes it may seem like there is no end in sight to the work involved in the job search. You might spend hours on end researching companies, revising your résumé, doing mock interviews, and submitting applications—all without hearing from any employers for months. Or you may have been to multiple job interviews without receiving a job offer. We've all been there. Rejection is part of the process, and it's a huge bummer.

Fortunately, you have an effective antidote to getting bummed out that most people don't have: your military training. Recall basic training. How did you get through it? It was as much a mental challenge as a physical challenge, right?

A recent article in *Time* magazine reported the U.S. military was implementing a resilience-building program designed by University of Pennsylvania researchers. Even if you haven't undergone the program, you'll appreciate these key points highlighted in the article:

1) "Mental toughness comes from thinking like an optimist." In other words, think of unemployment as a temporary circumstance. You have control over changing that situation and you'll eventually get yourself out of this rut.

2) Mental toughness comes from resisting "catastrophic thinking." Don't allow your thoughts to wander to the dark side. When you assume the worst is going to happen, it will.[31]

Tactical Patience

Think back to the first time you heard this: "Tactical patience does not rush the failure."

That quote struck me the first time I heard it during my many interviews with ex-military people. So I did some Internet research to find more references to fully understand the meaning of "tactical patience."

Here's a description from CWO2/Gunner Keith Marine in a 2010 blog post from *Foreign Policy* magazine, in which he spoke to reporter Thomas E. Ricks from Afghanistan:

> *We have done pretty well limiting civilian casualties but not as well as we could have if we observed a little longer—a couple is too many sometimes. A guy pulling a pitchfork out of the hay at night looks just like a guy taking a weapon out of a cache at first glance. Take the time to wait a few minutes and observe what the guys are doing before you shoot. The damage you cause may be irreparable. Along with that, if you are still covert and have the drop on folks, hold off. They may bring in some of their friends and you can kill them too.*

So it turns out that "tactical patience" is much more strategic and purposeful than the "regular patience" most civilians consider a

31 Annie Murphy Paul, "Can You Instill Mental Toughness?" *Time*, April 19, 2012, http://ideas.time.com/2012/04/19/can-you-instill-mental-toughness/.

virtue. As someone with a military background, real world experience has taught you the value of tactical patience. I urge you to keep that in mind as you trudge through the job search. If you make a snap decision to give up, you'll be causing irreparable damage.

Keep At It

If you remain diligent in your search, your work will pay off in the end. I guarantee it. I talked with Angel Faggins, field program support manager at the Military Personnel Services Corporation in California. She helps service members, veterans, and their dependants obtain full or part-time employment in careers within their specific skill sets. Angel has seen it all: people with inflexible job requirements, others who come in expecting her to do all the work, and those willing to put in the work to find a job.

She told me a story about a soldier who had returned from deployment facing incredibly rough personal circumstances. His wife had left him while he was on active duty and used all his money for mortgage payments. He was forced to live out of his car at an Army base. This guy was desperate for a job. He had had considerable leadership responsibilities in the Army and had been trained as a diesel mechanic.

Angel set him up with an interview at Kenai Drilling, a California-based company that provides drilling services for the exploration and development of oil, gas, and geothermal wells. However, he soon discovered he had an umbilical hernia that hadn't shown up in his military exit exam. His condition prevented him from getting the job with Kenai.

Still, this soldier persisted in his job search. He checked in with Angel every day and followed her advice consistently. Several weeks later, the same company offered him a job as a mud engineer managing drilling fluid. He had no experience as a mud engineer and was required to attend a thirty-day mud engineering training. According to Angel, he has done very well in his role and has since been promoted.

Angel advises job seekers to keep interacting with people. As I mentioned earlier, attend networking events and continue building the relationships you may have started at the beginning of your job search. Those live events give you opportunities to meet people, find support, and build a sense of camaraderie with others like you. They also help you refine your communication skills.

The worst thing job seekers can do is to isolate themselves. When you do that, whatever confidence you might have built up in the past can become deflated. And when that happens, you usually curtail your job search activity. I've seen it happen to many of my clients. They start out following my advice, set their weekly goals, stay busy, and feel like they're on top of their game. Then they land a job interview and have a good feeling about it, so they stop searching. As more time passes, they become increasingly more attached to that one job they interviewed for. When they don't hear back, they become depressed, angry, and hopeless. The negative feelings spread like wildfire, and it's nearly impossible to get them back on target.

Do Your Own After-Action Review (AAR)

Rejection often feels like an unexpected punch in the gut. You feel as though something happened to you that you simply couldn't control.

You must acknowledge and come to grips with the fact that you *will* face rejection and you *will* make mistakes. You *will* feel like a failure at times, and you *will* have your dark moments. Okay. So what's the worst that can happen?

- You submit hundreds of résumés, but no employers contact you.
- You bomb an interview.
- You spend a lot of time networking, but nobody you meet has the right connections to help you get a job.

These are not insurmountable problems. When you experience them first-hand, you become more of an expert at how tackle them. Throughout this book, I have referred to the job search as a process. It requires you to execute multiple actions for an extended period of time with a defined goal. Based on your successes and failures, you should continually be assessing your process and figuring out the techniques that work best for you.

I'm sure you are well acquainted with the AAR, which gives you and your unit an opportunity to discuss an event and identify what went wrong. It allows everyone to give candid insights on strengths and weaknesses from various perspectives. And it's a tremendous tool to get the maximum benefit out of every mission.[32]

Frustrated job seekers tend to worry, complain, and feed their misery. Don't let that happen to you. Conduct your own AAR. Strategize alone and with mentors, counselors, or recruiters on how to improve your action plan. Many times, you can make minor adjustments just by doing a self-evaluation of your routine. For example, are you in the habit of writing cover letters after dinner, when your energy is low and the kids are running around the house? Wake up two hours

32 "A Leader's Guide to After-Action Reviews," Training Circular 25-20, September 30, 1993, Headquarters, Department of the Army, accessed May 26, 2013, http://www.au.af.mil/au/awc/awcgate/army/tc_25-20/tc25-20.pdf.

earlier in the morning and write your cover letters while everyone else is sleeping. Are you having a difficult time finding networking events in your area? Maybe you have a brother or sister who lives in a metropolitan area two hours away. Look for networking events in that city and plan on spending the night at your sibling's apartment.

Take the time to do your AAR. Even minor adjustments can sometimes make a major difference. And remember, there are no mistakes in life, only lessons.

CHAPTER 8

Decommissioning to a Civilian Life

No one ever said that the transition from military to civilian life would be easy. One of the biggest lessons we learn in life is that change is inevitable. You can either position yourself to retreat or you can embrace the challenge and reap all the rewards.

Let me tell you a story about an ex-military candidate who submitted his résumé to me. Dave Gould was a thirty-nine-year-old father of two who had spent ten years in the Army. Dave had been a first sergeant with 350 people reporting to him. He didn't have a college degree, but he had taken some leadership courses in the Army.

When I met him, he had been working as an assembly technician making ten-gallon stainless steel chemical containers and valves. He found this position through a temp agency and was earning $14 per hour—a fraction of what he'd been making in the Army. The position was far from what he'd been searching for, but it was the only one he could get. Dave never intended to stay there permanently, so he reached out to me to help him find a better job.

When I asked Dave why he took the assembly technician job in the first place, he said, "I want to keep myself fresh and I want to provide for my family during that time as well. Also, I'm trying to learn as much as I possibly can."

During his time there, he learned valuable management systems widely used in manufacturing, including Six Sigma and Oracle Process Manufacturing. Dave had the right attitude, and from our first conversation, I knew I'd be able to help him. He was optimistic, strategic, and had turned his struggle into an opportunity. I later found out that Dave had saved up 184 days of paid leave in the military. Instead of taking a vacation, he went straight to work at the factory. Yes, Dave was grossly overqualified for the assembly technician job. He knew that, and I'm sure his family and friends knew that, too. Still, Dave used that job to give himself time to adjust to civilian life. And when he was ready to move on, he began his second job search.

I'm happy to report that I helped place Dave in a production supervisory position at a Fortune 500 food processing company. He manages thirty people and works long days. Fortunately, his ten years in the Army prepared him for the demands of production management.

Let Dave's story serve as an inspiration to you. If you keep the right perspective, you'll be able to use every experience to your advantage. Dave didn't take the low-paying assembly job begrudgingly or out of desperation. He was well aware that his brains and skills exceeded the minimum requirements of the job. He also knew he wouldn't be stuck making chemical containers forever. What differentiated him from many of the job candidates I meet is that he approached every day on the job as an opportunity to learn. He didn't stay home and sulk. He knew himself well enough to know that he needed time to adjust to civilian life. Despite the low pay and monotonous work, he still believed he was getting the most out of his experience. That perspective helped Dave succeed in the long run.

If you've done the exercises in this book and continue to set goals and work toward them, you should be pretty busy these days. But if you still find yourself moping around the house for weeks on end, consider one-day jobs. Why stay at home alone when you could be productive, earning a few bucks, and meeting people?

One-day jobs may not sound appealing, especially since you're coming from a place where you were entrusted with huge responsibility. One-day jobs are certainly not a long-term solution to unemployment. They typically pay about $9 per hour. Nevertheless, I truly believe that veterans can benefit significantly from short-term work. If you've been stuck at home, depressed for months because of your unemployment situation, you'd be surprised at how effectively these jobs—even for one day at low pay—can boost your morale.

Hirepatriots.com has a one-day job search engine specifically for military veterans and their spouses. The jobs are most often manual labor, such as landscaping, painting, carpentry, or minor repairs. Sometimes, they require helping people move or assist in home renovations. The job listings on this particular website are typically posted by homeowners who want to support ex-service members and older military veterans and their spouses who aren't able to do the work themselves.

The website's founder, Mark Baird, told me the most significant value of one-day jobs is meeting people. He shared an amazing story about one of the ex-servicemen who took a one-day job. The fellow was hired to assist at a banquet, set up the space, serve food, and clean up. At the end of the night, he sat down and had coffee and pie with a businessman who attended the event. They chatted for some time, and by the end of the conversation, the businessman was so impressed by what he had heard that he offered the vet a job.

If you think about it, short-term gigs could be part of the networking strategy discussed in earlier chapters. Let's say you set a goal to take a one-day manual labor job twice a week. By the end of the month, you will have met at least eight new people. That means you will have established a link to the professional, personal, familial, and academic networks of those eight people. Leave a lasting impression on your clients with your hard work, skills, and personality, and your one-day jobs could potentially connect you with others who can help you get full-time work.

It's not magic, folks. Opportunities are everywhere! You just have to stay positive, open-minded, and actively search for them. The success stories in this book didn't come from my imagination. They're real-life accounts. If you put the work into your job search, you will definitely have your own success story one day. In fact, I love hearing about these personal victories, and I personally encourage you to contact me at russ@directionalmotivation.com and share your story.

I certainly understand that the job hunt can be downright demoralizing at times. In the service, you were pushed beyond your limits physically, mentally, and emotionally. The missions you completed had tremendous consequences for millions of people. They might have made you feel invincible. But now, for many of you who are struggling to get a job, there will be times when you feel hopeless. Like Dave, you may be grossly overqualified for the positions you are presently able to secure, and that might leave you frustrated and stressed out.

Remember, your current unemployed status is merely temporary. In the future, you'll look back at this time as a rough spot you were eventually able to smooth out. You're in a transition phase, and **you are not alone**.

I hope that by now, you feel energized and empowered to change your circumstances. You have a lot of work ahead of you, but as Thomas Jefferson once said, "Nothing can stop the man with the right mental attitude from achieving his goal; nothing on earth can help the man with the wrong mental attitude."

AUTHOR'S NOTE

As I reflect back on this book and the numerous interviews I conducted with military veterans around the world, I humbly admit that I am unworthy. Unworthy of the bloodshed and lost lives. Unworthy of the sacrifices that you, our country's defenders and protectors, have made to allow people like me to live in a free country.

I am indebted to you, and my indebtedness was the driving force behind this book. My intent was not only to help military veterans succeed in finding employment, but also to spread awareness of the tremendous struggles military veterans face upon returning to the private sector. For so many of you, your lives will never be the same. You might be facing obstacles that seem overwhelming, but if you persist, you will come out on top.

In the early stages of writing this book, I considered it a side project. I began researching the topic through books about transitioning to civilian life after the military. But I noticed there were very few resources specifically geared to helping military veterans prepare mentally, physically, and emotionally for the job hunt. I realized that a book offering tailored guidance to veterans was vital. As

I talked to more veterans and heard their stories, I gained a deeper understanding of their struggles to secure employment, and I became determined to make a difference.

I trust that this book will provide a pivotal step for you as you move out of the military and join the ranks of us civilians. The transition will certainly not happen overnight. The employment search is an unpredictable, long-term engagement, but remember, your present situation is not permanent. Each day brings new opportunities.

In addition to this book, we created a website www.directionalmotivation.com that offers free resources to help veterans in their job search. I truly believe the unique strategies we offer will make a difference for you and your fellow military veterans.

My work can never come close to paying my debt to you, but I hope that my advice will make a positive impact on your life. This is my way of offering a heartfelt thank you.

However, my work is only as good as the impact I make in other people's lives. If you found this book to be helpful, please help me get the word out, so that others can benefit from it. I encourage you to share it with other veterans, service groups, colleges, civic groups, and through social media. I would also encourage you to submit your reviews online at Amazon and Barnes and Noble.

If you are an employer, take the time to think about how a military veteran can benefit your organization. America's heroes have demonstrated in the face of incredible odds that we can count on them. Before you hire that next employee, may I suggest that you interview a veteran? I'm sure you will find—as so many employers have—that those who have served in the armed forces have much to offer your organization.

Veterans, I wish you success in your job search. I'm confident that you have a bright future ahead. If I can be of assistance, please don't hesitate to e-mail me at russ@directionalmotivation.com.

In service to you,

Russ Hovendick, *Founder*
Directional Motivation

President
Client Staffing Solutions, Inc.

Directional Motivation was founded specifically to help people with interviewing skills, career counseling, webinars, books, live forums, webinars, scholarships and other resources. Visit us at www.directionalmotivation.com

Client Staffing Solutions, Inc. is a national search and placement firm with twenty years of industry experience. Our specialty areas include, but are not limited to, engineering, maintenance, manufacturing, production, packaging, logistics, sanitation, quality, operations, research and development, human resource management, sales and marketing, IT, and executive-level positions. Visit us at www.clientstaffingsolutions.com.

APPENDIX

Resources for Veterans

Army Career and Alumni Program (ACAP)
https://www.acap.army.mil/default.aspx

American Corporate Partners
http://www.acp-usa.org/

Association of the United States Army (AUSA)
http://careers.ausa.org/

CareerBuilder Report: Mission Critical
http://careerbuildercommunications.com/pdf/CareerBuilder_Mission-Critical.pdf
http://www.thevalueofaveteran.com/

Clearance Jobs
for U.S. citizens with active Federal security clearance
http://www.clearancejobs.com/

Employer Support of the Guard and Reserve (ESGR)
http://www.esgr.mil/

GI Jobs
http://www.gijobs.com/

Hero 2 Hired
Employer Partnership of the Armed Forces' job portal merged with the Office of the Secretary of Defense for Reserve Affairs' Hero 2 Hired, H2H, program
https://h2h.jobs/

Hire Heroes USA
http://www.hireheroesusa.org/

Hire Patriots
http://www.hirepatriots.com/

Hiring Our Heroes (a program of the U.S. Chamber of Commerce Foundation)
http://www.uschamber.com/hiringourheroes

Military.com/Monster Veteran Employment Center
http://www.military.com/veteran-jobs

Military Friendly
http://www.militaryfriendly.com/

Military Hire
http://www.militaryhire.com/

Military Officers Association of America (MOAA)
http://www.moaa.org/retiredstillworking/

Military Times Best for Vets 2013: Employers
http://projects.militarytimes.com/best-for-veterans/best-employers-for-veterans/2013/

Military Times Best for Vets: Colleges 2013
http://projects.militarytimes.com/jobs/best-for-vets/2013/colleges/4-year/

Recruit Military
http://recruitmilitary.com/

Reserve Officers Association/Corporate Gray Career Center
http://roa.corporategrayonline.com/

Six Sigma Wings for Heroes
Military and Veteran Lean Six Sigma Black Belt Training and Certification Scholarships
http://www.ssmimilitaryscholarship.com/

USAA Career Center
https://www.usaa.apply2jobs.com/profext/military_recruiting.html

Veterans Connect: http://www.veteransconnect.net/

Veterans Retraining Assistance Program (VRAP)
The VOW to Hire Heroes Act of 2011 includes a new program that helps a limited number of participants who are unemployed and enroll in full-time training programs for high-demand occupations. Participants in the Veterans Retraining Assistance Program (VRAP) receive up to a year of financial assistance equal to the monthly full-time pay rate under the GI Bill.
http://benefits.va.gov/vow/education.htm

Vet Jobs
https://vetjobs.com/

Resources for Military Veteran Entrepreneurs
Operation Boots to Business
http://boots2business.org

Small Business Administration Resources for Veterans
http://www.sba.gov/content/veteran-service-disabled-veteran-owned

Small Business Administration Veterans Business Outreach Centers
http://www.sba.gov/content/veterans-business-outreach-centers

Recommended Reading

Still Standing: The Story of SSG John Kriesel
By Jim Kosmo and John Kriesel

Out of Uniform: Your Guide to a Successful Military-to-Civilian Career Transition
Tom Wolfe

ABOUT THE AUTHOR

Russ Hovendick is a national award winning executive recruiter. For twenty years, he has motivated hundreds of people through his multiple roles as recruiter, career coach, training consultant, business owner, and volunteer chaplain/counselor within the juvenile, jail, and prison system of South Dakota.

He heads Client Staffing Solutions, Inc., an executive recruiting agency, and recently founded the Directional Motivation Group www.directionalmotivation.com which offers career development books, training, webinars, scholarships, veteran services, career and life coaching, and other resources dedicated to making a difference in people's lives. With his positive approach and energetic personality, he is a frequent guest on radio and TV stations. His Directional Motivation book series has been widely endorsed by business and educational leaders across the country.

For booking inquiries, you may contact Russ at russ@directionalmotivation.com.

If you enjoyed this book you may be interested in other books in the Directional Motivation series.

How to Get a Raise: The Correct Way to ask for an Increase in Salary and Wages

by Russ Hovendick

Book Summary: Taking a unique "Market Value" approach this book challenges the conventional wisdom of how to ask for a raise. Through the "3 P's" method, the reader is first encouraged to **P**repare their rationale for the raise through a system of self-assessments to determine their "Marketplace Value", then develop and refine their own **P**resentation of Value, and finally to embrace an attitude of **P**rofessionalism throughout the process. By incorporating the "No-risk" approach this book provides, the reader enters the pay discussion without risk of jeopardizing their career and future raise and promotional considerations. If you have ever wanted a surefire approach to asking for a raise, this is it.

How to interview: What employers want to hear in today's competitive job market

by Russ Hovendick

Book Summary: From the opening paragraph this book will challenge your preconceived ideas about the interviewing process, providing "Key" insights to help you prepare, capture the employer's attention, and close the deal. Using these unique methods you will now have the ability to significantly differentiate yourself from your competition. In a today's competitive employment marketplace, why not stack the odds in your favor?